Table Of Contents

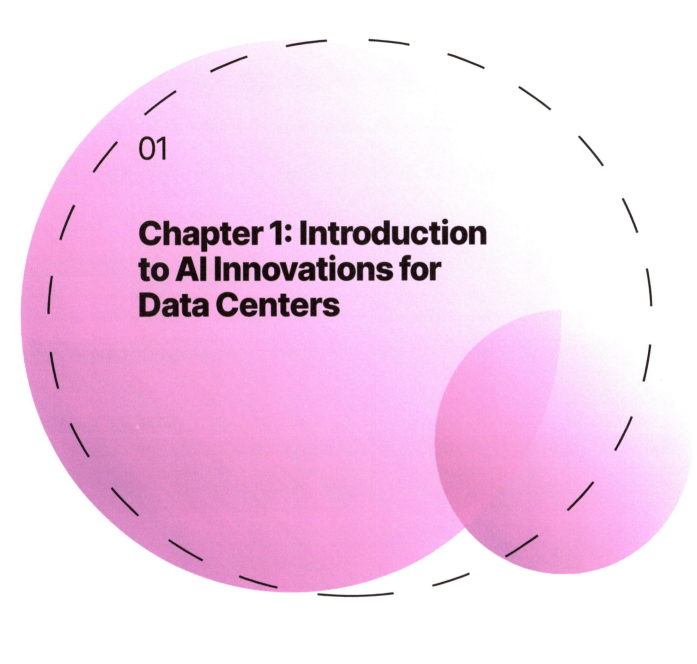

01

Chapter 1: Introduction to AI Innovations for Data Centers

The Role of AI in Data Centers

In today's digital age, data centers play a crucial role in storing, managing, and processing vast amounts of data. With the increasing complexity and scale of data center operations, the role of artificial intelligence (AI) has become more prominent than ever. AI technologies are revolutionizing the way data centers operate, offering a wide range of benefits from energy optimization to security monitoring and threat detection.

One of the key roles of AI in data centers is AI-powered energy optimization. By leveraging AI algorithms and machine learning techniques, data centers can intelligently manage their energy consumption and reduce costs. AI can analyze historical data, predict future energy demands, and automatically adjust cooling and power usage to optimize efficiency. This not only helps data centers save on energy bills but also contributes to a more sustainable and environmentally friendly operation.

Another important role of AI in data centers is AI-driven predictive maintenance for data center equipment. By utilizing AI-powered predictive analytics, data centers can proactively identify potential equipment failures before they occur. This helps prevent costly downtime and ensures the smooth operation of critical infrastructure. AI algorithms can analyze equipment performance data in real-time, detect anomalies, and provide recommendations for maintenance or replacement.

AI-based security monitoring and threat detection is also a critical role that AI plays in data centers. With the increasing sophistication of cyber threats, data centers must have robust security measures in place to protect sensitive data. AI technologies can analyze network traffic, detect unusual patterns or behaviors, and quickly respond to security incidents. By leveraging AI-driven threat detection, data centers can enhance their cybersecurity posture and mitigate the risk of cyber attacks.

AI-driven workload optimization and resource allocation is another key role of AI in data centers. By analyzing workloads, resource usage, and performance metrics, AI algorithms can dynamically allocate resources to meet changing demands. This ensures optimal performance and efficiency, even during peak usage periods. AI-powered workload optimization helps data centers maximize their resource utilization and improve overall operational efficiency.

In conclusion, the role of AI in data centers is multifaceted and essential for modern data center operations. From energy optimization to security monitoring, workload optimization, and beyond, AI technologies offer a wide range of benefits for data center professionals. By embracing AI innovations, data centers can enhance their efficiency, reliability, and security, ultimately providing a better experience for their users and customers.

Benefits of AI in Data Center Operations

In today's increasingly digital world, data centers play a crucial role in storing, processing, and managing vast amounts of information for businesses of all sizes. With the rise of artificial intelligence (AI) technology, data center operations are being revolutionized in ways that were previously thought impossible. In this subchapter, we will explore the numerous benefits that AI brings to data center operations, from energy optimization and predictive maintenance to security monitoring and workload optimization.

One of the key benefits of AI in data center operations is its ability to optimize energy usage. AI-powered energy optimization systems can analyze data center energy consumption patterns in real-time, identify areas of inefficiency, and make adjustments to reduce energy waste. This not only helps to lower operational costs but also reduces the environmental impact of data centers by minimizing their carbon footprint.

AI-driven predictive maintenance is another valuable application of AI technology in data centers. By analyzing data from various sensors and equipment, AI algorithms can predict when critical components are likely to fail and proactively schedule maintenance to prevent costly downtime. This proactive approach to maintenance helps data center professionals to optimize equipment performance and extend the lifespan of their hardware.

In terms of security, AI-based monitoring and threat detection systems offer data center professionals a powerful tool for safeguarding their infrastructure against cyber threats. These sophisticated AI algorithms can detect unusual patterns in network traffic, identify potential security breaches, and respond to threats in real-time, helping to protect sensitive data and prevent costly data breaches.

AI-driven workload optimization and resource allocation are essential for maximizing the efficiency of data center operations. By analyzing workload demands and resource availability, AI algorithms can dynamically adjust resource allocation to ensure optimal performance and minimize downtime. This agile approach to resource management helps data center professionals to meet the demands of their workloads while reducing operational costs.

In conclusion, the integration of AI technology into data center operations offers a wide range of benefits for professionals in the field. From energy optimization and predictive maintenance to security monitoring and workload optimization, AI technology is transforming the way data centers operate. By leveraging the power of AI, data center professionals can improve efficiency, enhance security, and optimize performance to meet the growing demands of today's digital world.

Overview of AI Technologies in Data Centers

In today's fast-paced digital world, data centers play a crucial role in storing, processing, and managing vast amounts of data. With the increasing complexity and scale of data centers, the need for efficient and intelligent solutions has become more important than ever. This has led to the integration of Artificial Intelligence (AI) technologies in data centers to optimize operations, improve energy efficiency, enhance security, and ensure seamless performance. One of the key areas where AI is making a significant impact in data centers is in energy optimization. AI-powered algorithms can analyze energy consumption patterns, predict peak loads, and optimize energy usage to reduce costs and minimize environmental impact. By leveraging AI technologies, data center operators can achieve substantial energy savings without compromising performance or reliability. Another critical application of AI in data centers is predictive maintenance for equipment. By utilizing AI-driven predictive analytics, data center operators can identify potential equipment failures before they occur, enabling proactive maintenance and minimizing downtime. This not only improves operational efficiency but also extends the lifespan of equipment, resulting in cost savings and enhanced reliability.

Security monitoring and threat detection are also areas where AI technologies are revolutionizing data center operations. AI-based security systems can analyze massive amounts of data in real-time, identify anomalies, and detect potential security threats before they escalate. This advanced level of threat detection helps data center operators to strengthen their security posture and protect sensitive data from cyber-attacks. Workload optimization and resource allocation are crucial for ensuring optimal performance and efficiency in data centers. AI-driven algorithms can analyze workload patterns, predict resource requirements, and dynamically allocate resources to meet demand. This intelligent resource management not only improves performance but also maximizes utilization and minimizes wastage, resulting in cost savings and operational efficiency.

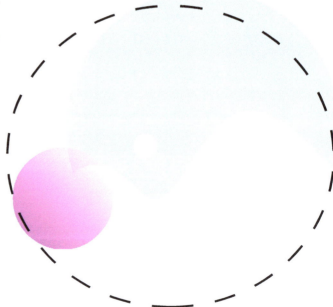

Overall, AI technologies are transforming every aspect of data center operations, from cooling and environmental control systems to capacity planning and scalability solutions. By harnessing the power of AI, data center professionals can enhance performance, increase efficiency, improve security, and drive innovation in their operations. As the technology continues to evolve, the possibilities for AI-powered solutions in data centers are limitless, offering unprecedented opportunities for professionals in the industry to optimize their operations and stay ahead of the competition.

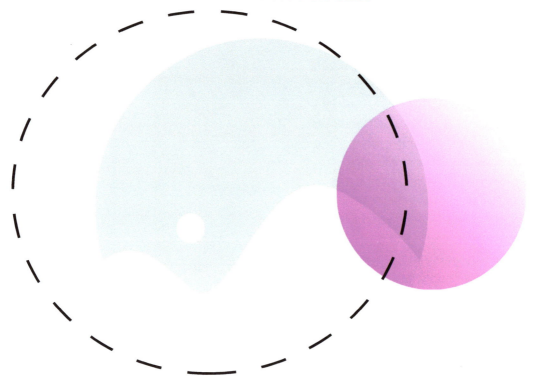

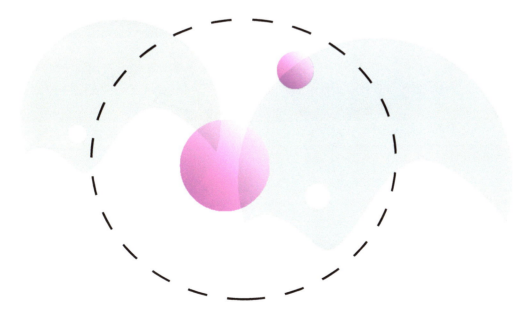

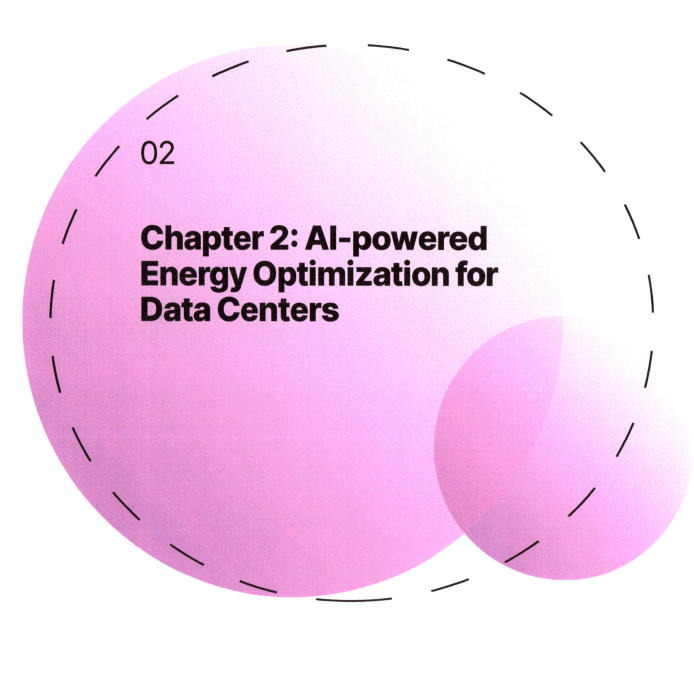

02

Chapter 2: AI-powered Energy Optimization for Data Centers

Energy Efficiency in Data Centers

Data centers play a crucial role in today's business landscape, serving as the backbone for storing, processing, and managing vast amounts of data. However, data centers are also notorious for their high energy consumption, accounting for a significant portion of overall energy usage globally. As such, the need for energy efficiency in data centers has become a top priority for professionals in the field.

AI innovations have emerged as a game-changer in the quest for energy efficiency in data centers. By leveraging AI algorithms and machine learning techniques, data center operators can optimize energy usage, reduce waste, and lower operational costs. AI-powered energy optimization solutions can dynamically adjust power usage based on workload demands, temperature fluctuations, and other factors to ensure maximum efficiency.

In addition to energy optimization, AI-driven predictive maintenance is another key area where AI innovations are making a significant impact in data centers. By analyzing historical data, monitoring equipment performance in real-time, and predicting potential failures, AI algorithms can help prevent costly downtime and extend the lifespan of critical data center equipment.

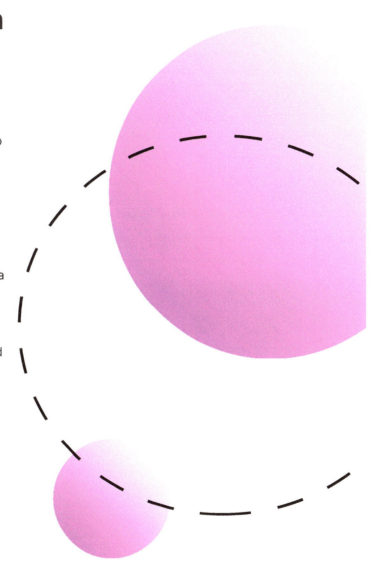

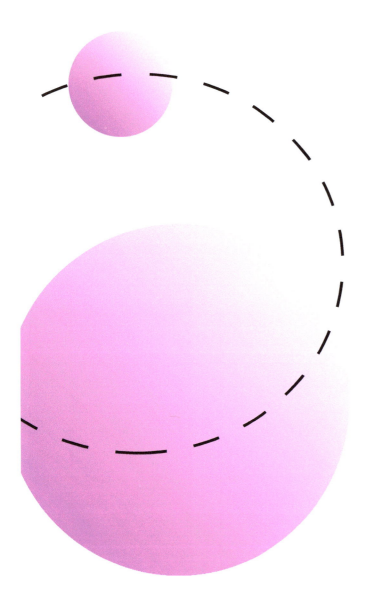

Furthermore, AI-based security monitoring and threat detection solutions are essential for safeguarding data centers against cyber threats and unauthorized access. By continuously monitoring network traffic, detecting anomalies, and identifying potential security breaches, AI-powered security solutions can proactively protect sensitive data and ensure compliance with regulatory requirements.

AI-driven workload optimization and resource allocation are also critical for maximizing the efficiency and performance of data centers. By analyzing workload patterns, predicting resource demands, and dynamically allocating resources based on real-time data, AI algorithms can ensure optimal performance while minimizing energy consumption and operational costs. Overall, AI innovations are revolutionizing the way data centers operate, enabling professionals to achieve unprecedented levels of energy efficiency, security, and performance.

AI Techniques for Energy Optimization

AI techniques are revolutionizing the way data centers manage their energy consumption and optimize their operations. By leveraging artificial intelligence, data center professionals can achieve significant energy savings and improve overall efficiency. In this subchapter, we will explore the various AI techniques that can be used for energy optimization in data centers.

One of the key AI techniques for energy optimization in data centers is predictive maintenance. By using machine learning algorithms to analyze equipment performance data, data center professionals can predict when maintenance is needed before a failure occurs. This proactive approach not only reduces downtime but also helps optimize energy usage by ensuring that equipment is operating at peak efficiency.

Another important AI technique for energy optimization in data centers is workload optimization and resource allocation. By using AI algorithms to analyze workloads and allocate resources accordingly, data center professionals can ensure that energy is being used efficiently. This approach can help reduce energy waste and lower overall operating costs.

AI-powered cooling and environmental control systems are also essential for energy optimization in data centers. By using AI algorithms to monitor and adjust cooling systems based on real-time data, data center professionals can ensure that energy is being used effectively to maintain optimal operating temperatures. This can result in significant energy savings and improved overall performance.

Furthermore, AI-based anomaly detection and performance monitoring are crucial for identifying energy inefficiencies in data centers. By using machine learning algorithms to analyze performance data and detect anomalies, data center professionals can quickly identify and address issues that may be impacting energy consumption. This proactive approach can help optimize energy usage and improve overall efficiency.

In conclusion, AI techniques offer data center professionals a powerful set of tools for energy optimization. By leveraging predictive maintenance, workload optimization, cooling systems, anomaly detection, and performance monitoring, data centers can achieve significant energy savings and improve overall efficiency. As the demand for data center services continues to grow, AI techniques will play an increasingly important role in helping data centers meet their energy optimization goals.

Case Studies on AI-powered Energy Optimization

In this subchapter, we will explore various case studies on AI-powered energy optimization in data centers. Energy optimization is a crucial aspect of data center management, as these facilities consume a significant amount of electricity to power and cool the servers and equipment. By leveraging AI technologies, data center professionals can achieve significant cost savings and improve operational efficiency. One case study focuses on a large data center that implemented AI-powered predictive maintenance for its equipment. By analyzing historical data and monitoring real-time performance metrics, the AI system was able to identify potential equipment failures before they occurred. This proactive approach not only reduced downtime but also optimized energy usage by ensuring that equipment was operating at peak efficiency.

Another case study showcases a data center that used AI-based security monitoring and threat detection to enhance its cybersecurity measures. The AI system continuously analyzed network traffic and user behavior to detect anomalies and potential security threats. By identifying and mitigating security risks in real-time, the data center was able to safeguard its critical infrastructure and prevent costly data breaches.

Furthermore, a case study on AI-driven workload optimization and resource allocation demonstrates how data centers can efficiently allocate computing resources based on workload demands. By analyzing workload patterns and performance metrics, the AI system dynamically adjusts resource allocation to ensure optimal performance and energy efficiency. This approach not only improves overall system performance but also reduces energy consumption and operational costs.

Moreover, a case study on AI-powered cooling and environmental control systems highlights the importance of maintaining optimal temperature and humidity levels in data centers. By utilizing AI algorithms to analyze environmental data and adjust cooling systems accordingly, data centers can achieve significant energy savings while ensuring optimal operating conditions for servers and equipment. This proactive approach to environmental control not only reduces energy waste but also extends the lifespan of critical infrastructure.

In conclusion, these case studies illustrate the diverse applications of AI technologies in energy optimization for data centers. By leveraging AI-driven solutions for predictive maintenance, security monitoring, workload optimization, and environmental control, data center professionals can enhance operational efficiency, reduce energy consumption, and improve overall system performance. As AI continues to evolve, data centers can expect even greater advancements in energy optimization and cost savings.

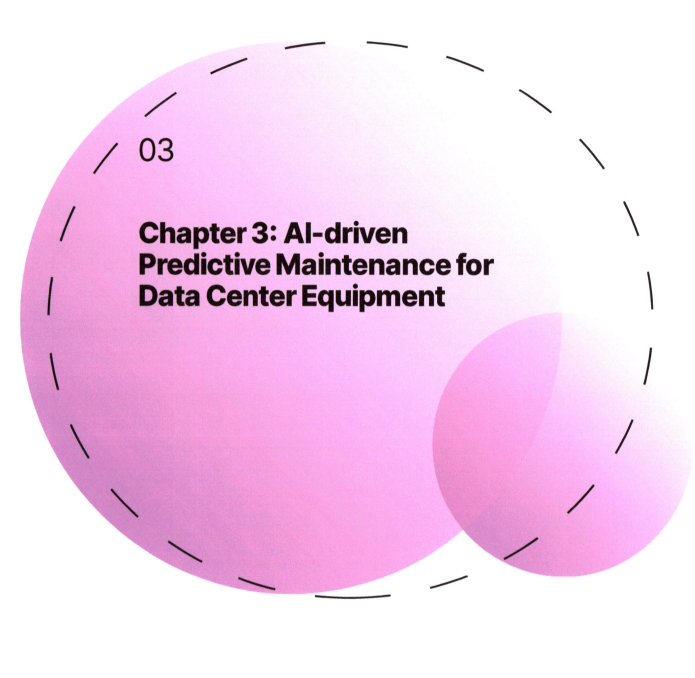

03

Chapter 3: AI-driven Predictive Maintenance for Data Center Equipment

Importance of Predictive Maintenance in Data Centers

In the fast-paced world of data centers, where downtime can cost companies millions of dollars, predictive maintenance has emerged as a critical tool for ensuring the smooth operation of equipment and minimizing the risk of unexpected failures. By leveraging artificial intelligence (AI) technologies, data center professionals can proactively identify and address potential issues before they escalate into costly outages.

One of the key benefits of predictive maintenance in data centers is the ability to optimize energy usage. By analyzing historical data and patterns, AI algorithms can predict when equipment is likely to fail or require maintenance, allowing operators to schedule downtime during off-peak hours and reduce energy consumption during peak times. This not only helps to lower operational costs but also contributes to a more sustainable and environmentally friendly data center operation.

Furthermore, AI-driven predictive maintenance can enhance security monitoring and threat detection within data centers. By continuously analyzing network traffic, user behavior, and system logs, AI algorithms can detect anomalies and potential security breaches in real-time, enabling operators to respond swiftly and effectively to mitigate risks. This proactive approach to cybersecurity is essential in safeguarding sensitive data and ensuring the integrity of the data center infrastructure.

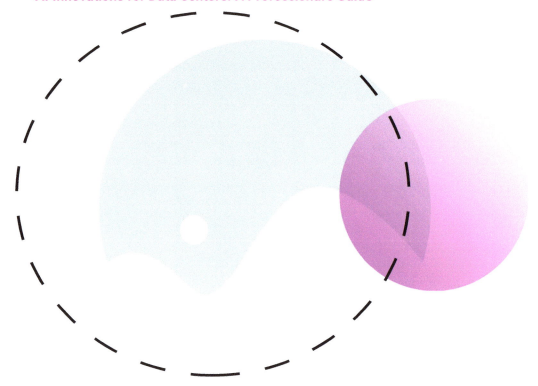

In addition to improving security and energy efficiency, predictive maintenance powered by AI can also optimize workload allocation and resource utilization in data centers. By analyzing performance metrics and demand patterns, AI algorithms can dynamically allocate resources to workload instances based on their requirements, ensuring optimal performance and resource utilization. This not only improves the overall efficiency of the data center but also enhances the user experience by minimizing latency and downtime.

Overall, the importance of predictive maintenance in data centers cannot be overstated. By leveraging AI technologies to proactively monitor, analyze, and optimize equipment performance, data center professionals can ensure the reliability, security, and efficiency of their operations. As the demand for data processing and storage continues to grow, predictive maintenance will play a crucial role in enabling data centers to meet the evolving needs of businesses and consumers in a cost-effective and sustainable manner.

AI Algorithms for Predictive Maintenance

In the rapidly evolving world of data centers, the implementation of artificial intelligence (AI) algorithms for predictive maintenance has become a game-changer for professionals in the industry. By leveraging AI technology, data center operators can proactively monitor and maintain their equipment to prevent costly downtime and ensure optimal performance.

AI-powered predictive maintenance utilizes advanced algorithms to analyze data from sensors and other sources to predict when equipment is likely to fail. By detecting potential issues before they occur, data center operators can schedule maintenance tasks at the most convenient times, minimizing disruption to operations. This proactive approach can significantly reduce unplanned downtime and increase the overall reliability of the data center infrastructure.

One of the key benefits of AI-driven predictive maintenance is its ability to optimize energy usage in data centers. By monitoring equipment performance and energy consumption patterns, AI algorithms can identify opportunities for energy efficiency improvements. This can lead to significant cost savings for data center operators, as well as a reduced environmental impact.

Furthermore, AI-based security monitoring and threat detection play a crucial role in safeguarding data center assets from cyber threats. By analyzing network traffic and system logs in real-time, AI algorithms can detect suspicious activities and potential security breaches before they cause harm. This proactive approach to cybersecurity is essential for protecting sensitive data and maintaining the trust of customers.

Overall, AI algorithms for predictive maintenance offer a wide range of benefits for professionals in the data center industry. From optimizing energy usage to enhancing security monitoring and threat detection, AI technology is revolutionizing the way data centers operate. By embracing these innovations, data center operators can stay ahead of the curve and ensure their infrastructure remains reliable, efficient, and secure.

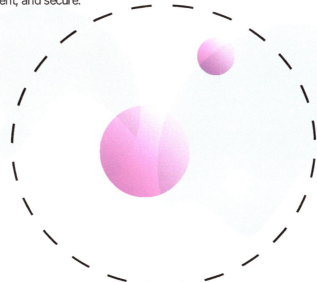

Implementing AI-driven Predictive Maintenance

Implementing AI-driven predictive maintenance in data centers is crucial for ensuring the seamless operation of equipment and preventing costly downtime. By leveraging artificial intelligence technology, data center professionals can proactively monitor the health of their equipment and address potential issues before they escalate into major problems. This subchapter will explore the benefits of AI-driven predictive maintenance and provide practical tips for implementing this innovative approach in data center environments.

One of the key advantages of AI-driven predictive maintenance is its ability to analyze vast amounts of data in real-time to identify patterns and anomalies that may indicate impending equipment failures. By collecting data from sensors and monitoring systems, AI algorithms can predict when a piece of equipment is likely to malfunction and alert data center operators to take preventive action. This proactive approach can help organizations avoid costly downtime, reduce maintenance costs, and extend the lifespan of their equipment.

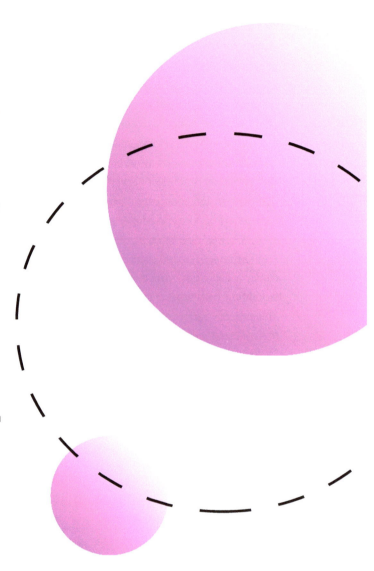

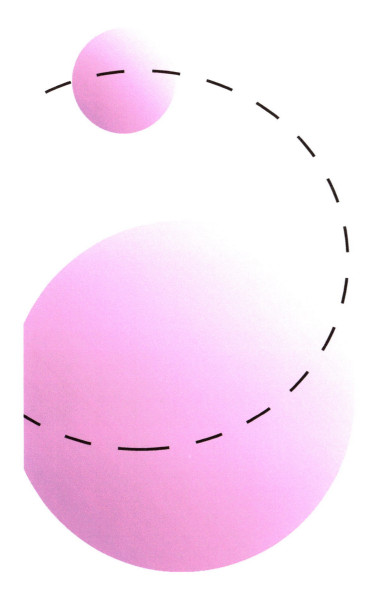

To successfully implement AI-driven predictive maintenance in data centers, professionals should first assess their current monitoring and maintenance practices to identify areas for improvement. This may involve upgrading existing sensors and monitoring systems to collect more granular data, integrating AI algorithms into monitoring software, or investing in predictive maintenance tools specifically designed for data center environments. By taking a holistic approach to predictive maintenance, data center professionals can create a more resilient and efficient infrastructure that is better equipped to handle the demands of modern IT environments.

Another important consideration when implementing AI-driven predictive maintenance in data centers is ensuring data security and privacy. As AI algorithms rely on large amounts of data to make accurate predictions, it is essential for organizations to establish robust data governance policies and practices to protect sensitive information. This may involve encrypting data, implementing access controls, and regularly auditing data storage and processing practices to ensure compliance with industry regulations and best practices.

In conclusion, AI-driven predictive maintenance offers data center professionals a powerful tool for optimizing equipment performance, reducing downtime, and improving overall operational efficiency. By leveraging AI technology to proactively monitor equipment health and predict potential failures, organizations can take a proactive approach to maintenance and ensure the uninterrupted operation of their data center infrastructure. With careful planning, implementation, and monitoring, data center professionals can harness the power of AI to transform their maintenance practices and drive greater value from their IT investments.

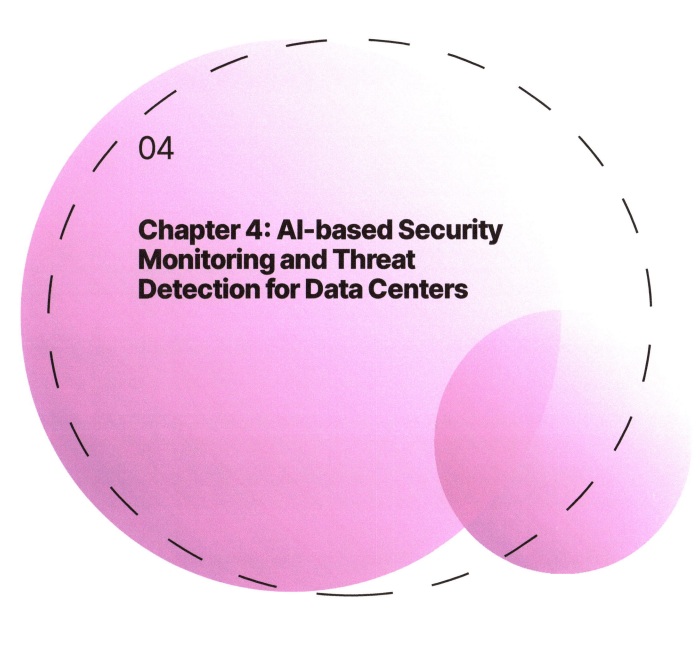

04

Chapter 4: AI-based Security Monitoring and Threat Detection for Data Centers

Cybersecurity Challenges in Data Centers

In recent years, data centers have become a prime target for cyber attacks due to the valuable and sensitive information they house. As technology continues to advance, so do the methods used by malicious actors to breach security measures. This has led to a number of cybersecurity challenges that data centers must address in order to protect their operations and data.

One of the primary challenges facing data centers is the increasing complexity of cyber threats. With the rise of artificial intelligence and machine learning, hackers are able to launch more sophisticated and targeted attacks that can evade traditional security measures. This means that data centers must constantly adapt and improve their cybersecurity defenses to stay ahead of these evolving threats.

Another major challenge is the sheer volume of data that data centers must protect. As the amount of data generated and stored by organizations continues to grow, so does the potential attack surface for cyber criminals. This means that data centers must implement robust security measures to safeguard this data and prevent unauthorized access or data breaches.

Additionally, data centers face challenges related to compliance and regulatory requirements. Many industries have strict data protection regulations that data centers must adhere to, such as the General Data Protection Regulation (GDPR) in Europe. Failure to comply with these regulations can result in hefty fines and damage to a data center's reputation.

Overall, cybersecurity challenges in data centers require a multi-faceted approach that combines advanced technologies such as artificial intelligence with stringent security protocols and proactive monitoring. By staying vigilant and continuously improving their cybersecurity defenses, data centers can mitigate the risks posed by cyber threats and ensure the safety and security of their operations and data.

AI Solutions for Security Monitoring

AI solutions for security monitoring in data centers have become increasingly crucial in today's digital landscape. With the rise of cyber threats and attacks, it is essential for professionals in the field to implement advanced AI technologies to safeguard their data centers. AI-powered security monitoring systems can analyze vast amounts of data in real-time, detecting anomalies and potential threats before they escalate into major security breaches.

One of the key benefits of using AI for security monitoring in data centers is its ability to automate threat detection and response processes. Traditional security monitoring systems rely on manual intervention, which can be time-consuming and prone to human error. AI solutions, on the other hand, can continuously monitor network traffic, identify suspicious patterns, and take immediate action to mitigate security risks. This proactive approach is essential for protecting sensitive data and ensuring the smooth operation of data center infrastructure. AI-driven security monitoring systems also offer predictive capabilities, allowing professionals to anticipate potential security threats and vulnerabilities before they occur. By analyzing historical data and identifying patterns of suspicious behavior, AI algorithms can help data center operators stay one step ahead of cyber attackers. This predictive approach not only enhances the overall security posture of the data center but also minimizes the impact of security incidents on business operations.

Furthermore, AI solutions for security monitoring can enhance the scalability and efficiency of data center operations. By automating routine security tasks and streamlining incident response processes, professionals can focus on more strategic initiatives and optimize resource allocation. This improved operational efficiency not only reduces the workload on IT teams but also enables data centers to adapt to changing security threats and business requirements.

In conclusion, AI-powered security monitoring solutions are essential for professionals in the data center industry to protect their infrastructure from cyber threats and ensure the continuity of business operations. By leveraging advanced AI technologies, professionals can enhance the security posture of their data centers, automate threat detection and response processes, and optimize operational efficiency. As the digital landscape continues to evolve, it is imperative for professionals to embrace AI innovations and stay ahead of emerging security challenges in data center environments.

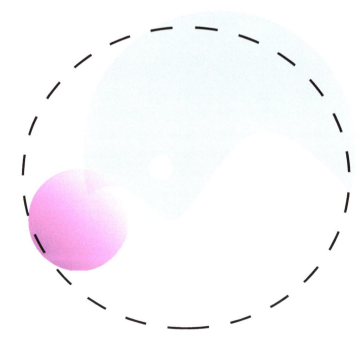

Detecting and Mitigating Threats with AI

In the fast-paced world of data centers, staying ahead of potential threats is crucial to maintaining optimal performance and security. With the rise of artificial intelligence (AI), professionals now have powerful tools at their disposal to detect and mitigate threats in real-time. In this subchapter, we will explore how AI can revolutionize threat detection and mitigation in data centers, providing professionals with the insights and solutions needed to safeguard their operations.

AI for data centers offers a proactive approach to threat detection by analyzing vast amounts of data in real-time to identify patterns and anomalies that may indicate a potential threat. By leveraging machine learning algorithms, AI can quickly detect and respond to security breaches, unauthorized access attempts, and other malicious activities before they escalate. This proactive approach not only enhances security but also minimizes downtime and potential damage to critical systems.

AI-powered energy optimization for data centers is another key aspect of threat detection and mitigation. By analyzing energy consumption patterns and identifying areas of inefficiency, AI can help data center professionals optimize their energy usage, reduce costs, and minimize the environmental impact of their operations. This not only improves sustainability but also enhances overall operational efficiency and reliability.

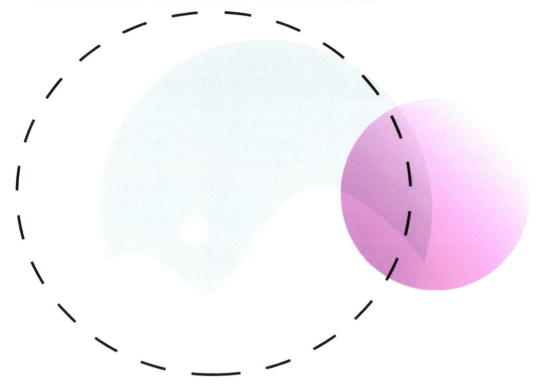

AI-driven predictive maintenance for data center equipment is essential for preventing costly downtime and equipment failures. By analyzing historical data and performance metrics, AI can predict when equipment is likely to fail and proactively schedule maintenance to prevent disruptions. This proactive approach not only extends the lifespan of equipment but also reduces the risk of catastrophic failures that could impact data center operations.

AI-based security monitoring and threat detection for data centers go hand in hand, providing professionals with the tools needed to monitor network traffic, detect suspicious activities, and respond to security incidents in real-time. By analyzing vast amounts of data and identifying potential threats, AI can help data center professionals stay one step ahead of cybercriminals and protect their critical assets from harm. This proactive approach to security monitoring is essential for safeguarding data centers against evolving threats in today's digital landscape.

In conclusion, AI offers a powerful set of tools for detecting and mitigating threats in data centers, providing professionals with the insights and solutions needed to safeguard their operations. By leveraging AI for energy optimization, predictive maintenance, security monitoring, and threat detection, data center professionals can enhance operational efficiency, reliability, and security, ensuring the continued success of their operations in an increasingly complex and dynamic environment.

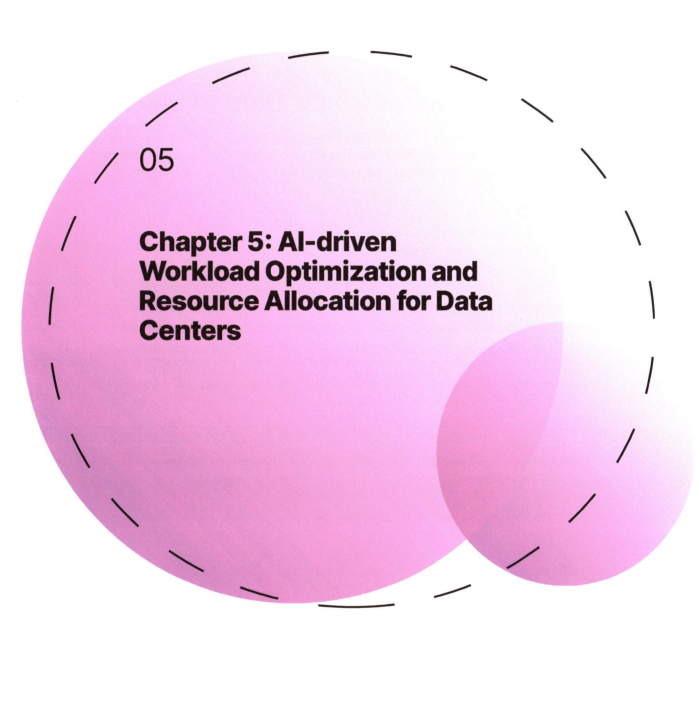

05

Chapter 5: AI-driven Workload Optimization and Resource Allocation for Data Centers

Workload Management in Data Centers

Workload management in data centers is a critical aspect of ensuring optimal performance and efficiency. With the increasing complexity of data center environments and the growing demand for processing power, it has become essential for data center professionals to effectively manage workloads to meet the needs of their organizations. AI innovations have revolutionized workload management in data centers, providing professionals with powerful tools to optimize resource allocation and improve overall performance.

AI-powered workload optimization and resource allocation solutions are designed to intelligently distribute workloads across servers and infrastructure to ensure optimal performance. By analyzing data in real-time and predicting workload patterns, AI algorithms can dynamically allocate resources to meet changing demands. This not only improves performance but also helps to reduce energy consumption and operational costs. Professionals can leverage AI-driven workload optimization tools to maximize the efficiency of their data center operations and ensure seamless service delivery to end-users.

In addition to workload optimization, AI innovations are also being used for predictive maintenance of data center equipment. By analyzing data from sensors and monitoring equipment, AI algorithms can detect potential issues before they occur, allowing professionals to proactively address maintenance needs and prevent costly downtime. This predictive maintenance approach not only improves the reliability of data center equipment but also extends its lifespan, ultimately reducing operational costs and enhancing overall efficiency.

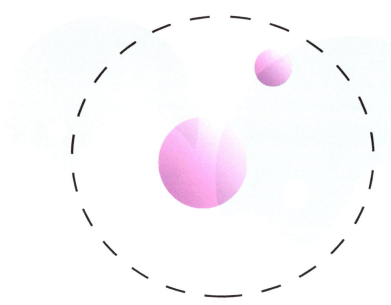

AI-based security monitoring and threat detection solutions are another critical component of workload management in data centers. With the increasing number of cyber threats and security breaches targeting data centers, professionals need advanced tools to monitor network traffic, detect anomalies, and respond to potential security incidents. AI-powered security solutions leverage machine learning algorithms to detect suspicious activities and identify potential threats in real-time, enabling professionals to take immediate action to protect their data center environment. Overall, AI innovations have transformed workload management in data centers, providing professionals with powerful tools to optimize resource allocation, improve equipment maintenance, enhance security monitoring, and ensure seamless service delivery. By leveraging AI-driven solutions, professionals can maximize the efficiency of their data center operations, reduce operational costs, and provide a secure and reliable environment for their organizations. As data center environments continue to evolve, AI will play an increasingly important role in workload management, helping professionals to meet the growing demands of their organizations and deliver high-performance services to end-users.

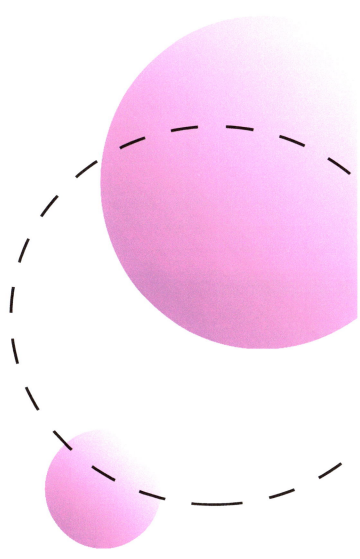

AI Approaches for Resource Allocation

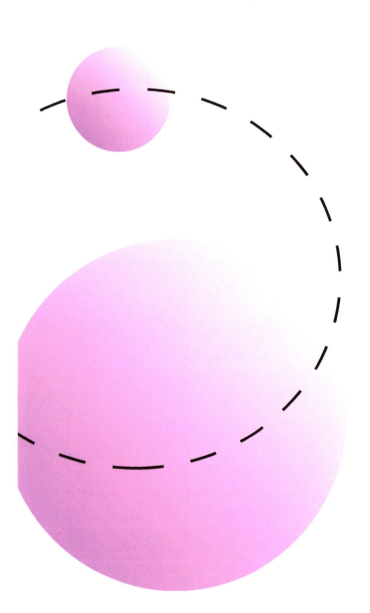

In the fast-paced and constantly evolving world of data centers, efficient resource allocation is crucial for maximizing performance and minimizing costs. Artificial Intelligence (AI) has emerged as a powerful tool for optimizing resource allocation in data centers, enabling professionals to make data-driven decisions that enhance efficiency and productivity.

One key AI approach for resource allocation in data centers is AI-driven workload optimization. By analyzing historical data and real-time performance metrics, AI algorithms can intelligently distribute workloads across servers to ensure optimal utilization of resources. This not only improves overall efficiency but also helps in preventing bottlenecks and downtime, leading to enhanced performance and user satisfaction.

Another important application of AI in resource allocation is AI-based cooling and environmental control systems. By leveraging AI algorithms to monitor and adjust temperature, humidity, and airflow in data centers, professionals can ensure that servers operate within optimal conditions, reducing energy consumption and extending the lifespan of equipment. This not only results in cost savings but also contributes to a more sustainable and environmentally friendly data center operation.

AI-powered data center capacity planning and scalability solutions are also essential for efficient resource allocation. By analyzing data trends and predicting future needs, AI algorithms can help professionals in planning for future capacity requirements and scaling resources accordingly. This proactive approach not only ensures smooth operations but also helps in avoiding costly over-provisioning or under-provisioning of resources.

AI-based anomaly detection and performance monitoring play a critical role in resource allocation by identifying abnormalities and potential issues in data center operations. By continuously monitoring performance metrics and detecting anomalies in real-time, professionals can quickly address issues and allocate resources effectively to prevent downtime and ensure optimal performance. This proactive approach helps in maintaining high availability and reliability of data center services.

In conclusion, AI-driven resource allocation is a game-changer for data centers, enabling professionals to optimize performance, reduce costs, and enhance reliability. By leveraging AI approaches such as workload optimization, cooling and environmental control, capacity planning, and anomaly detection, professionals can make informed decisions that lead to efficient resource allocation and improved overall data center operations. With the rapid advancements in AI technology, the future of resource allocation in data centers looks promising, with endless possibilities for innovation and optimization.

Optimizing Workload Performance with AI

In today's fast-paced and highly competitive business landscape, data centers play a crucial role in ensuring the seamless operation of critical applications and services. As the demand for data processing and storage continues to grow, data center professionals are constantly faced with the challenge of optimizing workload performance to meet the needs of their organizations. Fortunately, advancements in artificial intelligence (AI) technology have opened up new possibilities for enhancing the efficiency and effectiveness of data center operations.

One area where AI is making a significant impact is in workload optimization and resource allocation. By leveraging machine learning algorithms, data center operators can now analyze historical workload data and predict future resource requirements with a high degree of accuracy. This allows them to dynamically allocate resources based on real-time demand, ensuring optimal performance and minimizing wastage. In addition, AI-powered workload optimization can help data centers achieve higher levels of efficiency, reduce operational costs, and improve overall system performance.

Another key application of AI in data centers is predictive maintenance for equipment. By analyzing sensor data and performance metrics in real-time, AI algorithms can identify potential issues before they escalate into costly downtime or equipment failures. This proactive approach to maintenance not only extends the lifespan of critical infrastructure but also improves the overall reliability and availability of data center services. With AI-driven predictive maintenance, data center professionals can schedule maintenance tasks more efficiently, reduce unplanned outages, and optimize the performance of their equipment.

In the realm of security monitoring and threat detection, AI is proving to be a game-changer for data center operators. By analyzing vast amounts of network traffic and log data, AI algorithms can quickly identify suspicious behavior, detect anomalies, and respond to security threats in real-time. This proactive approach to security not only enhances the overall resilience of data center environments but also helps organizations stay ahead of evolving cyber threats. With AI-based security monitoring, data center professionals can strengthen their defense mechanisms, mitigate risks, and safeguard critical assets from potential breaches.

Furthermore, AI technologies are also being utilized to improve cooling and environmental control systems in data centers. By analyzing temperature and humidity data, AI algorithms can optimize cooling strategies, balance airflow, and reduce energy consumption without compromising performance. This not only helps data centers achieve greater energy efficiency and reduce operating costs but also minimizes the environmental impact of their operations. With AI-powered cooling solutions, data center operators can create more sustainable and environmentally friendly infrastructure that meets the needs of today's digital economy.

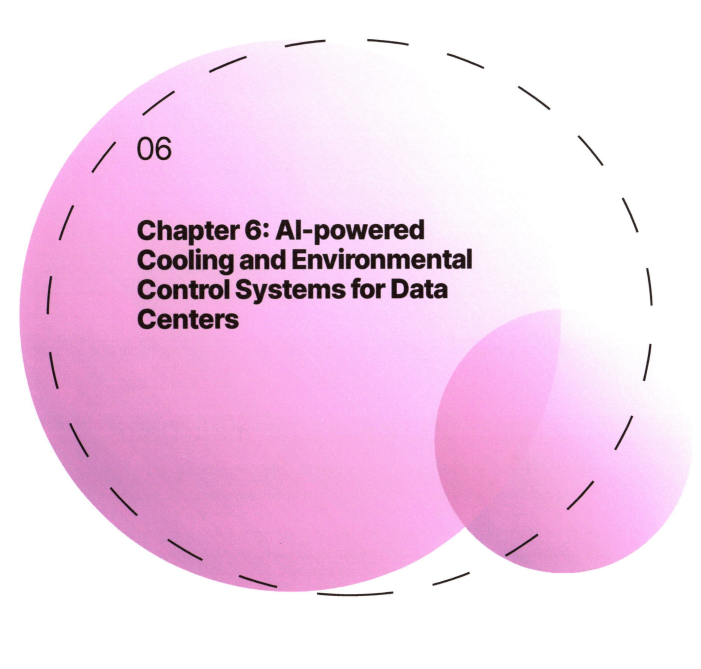

06

Chapter 6: AI-powered Cooling and Environmental Control Systems for Data Centers

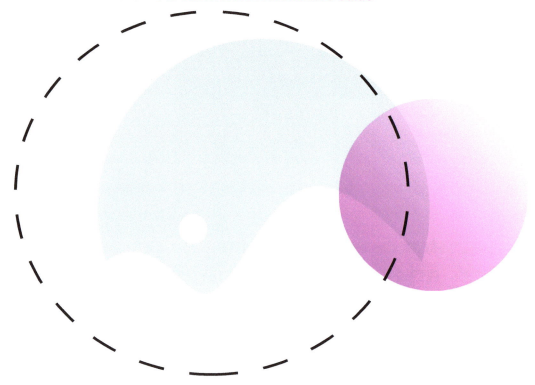

Importance of Cooling Systems in Data Centers

In the fast-paced world of data centers, ensuring optimal performance and efficiency is crucial for businesses to stay competitive. One key component that plays a vital role in maintaining the smooth operation of data centers is cooling systems. The importance of cooling systems in data centers cannot be overstated, as they are responsible for regulating the temperature and humidity levels to prevent overheating and potential damage to valuable equipment.

AI-powered cooling systems are revolutionizing the way data centers are managed, offering more precise and efficient control over environmental conditions. By utilizing advanced algorithms and machine learning capabilities, AI can analyze real-time data and adjust cooling settings accordingly to optimize energy consumption and reduce operational costs. This not only improves the overall performance of data centers but also extends the lifespan of equipment by preventing overheating and potential breakdowns.

Furthermore, AI-driven predictive maintenance for cooling systems can help data center professionals anticipate and address potential issues before they escalate into costly downtime. By monitoring equipment performance and analyzing historical data, AI algorithms can detect early warning signs of malfunctions and recommend proactive maintenance actions to prevent system failures. This proactive approach not only minimizes the risk of unexpected downtime but also maximizes the efficiency and reliability of cooling systems.

In addition, AI-powered security monitoring and threat detection systems can enhance the overall security posture of data centers by identifying and mitigating potential threats in real-time. By analyzing network traffic patterns and identifying anomalies, AI algorithms can detect suspicious activities and alert security teams to take immediate action. This proactive approach to security not only protects sensitive data and critical infrastructure but also ensures the continuity of business operations in the face of cyber threats.

Overall, AI innovations in cooling systems play a crucial role in optimizing the performance, efficiency, and security of data centers. By leveraging the power of AI for data center management, professionals can enhance the resilience and scalability of their infrastructure while reducing operational costs and mitigating risks. As data centers continue to evolve and grow in complexity, embracing AI-driven solutions for cooling systems is essential for staying ahead of the curve and achieving sustainable success in the digital age.

AI Applications in Environmental Control

Artificial Intelligence (AI) has revolutionized the way data centers operate, offering innovative solutions to improve efficiency, reduce energy consumption, and enhance overall performance. One of the key applications of AI in data centers is environmental control. AI-powered cooling and environmental control systems play a crucial role in maintaining optimal conditions for data center equipment, ensuring reliable operation and preventing overheating.

AI algorithms can analyze data from temperature sensors, humidity levels, and airflow patterns to optimize cooling systems in real-time. By predicting potential hotspots and adjusting cooling settings accordingly, AI can prevent equipment failures and downtime. This proactive approach to environmental control not only improves equipment reliability but also reduces energy consumption, leading to significant cost savings for data center operators.

In addition to cooling systems, AI can also be used to monitor and optimize other environmental factors such as air quality and noise levels in data centers. By collecting and analyzing data from various sensors, AI algorithms can detect anomalies and alert operators to potential issues before they escalate. This proactive approach to environmental monitoring helps maintain a healthy and safe working environment for data center staff while ensuring optimal conditions for equipment operation.

Furthermore, AI-driven data center capacity planning and scalability solutions can help operators optimize resource allocation and plan for future growth. By analyzing historical data and predicting future demand, AI algorithms can recommend the most efficient use of resources, such as server virtualization and consolidation. This not only improves performance and reduces costs but also ensures that data centers can scale up or down as needed to meet changing business requirements.

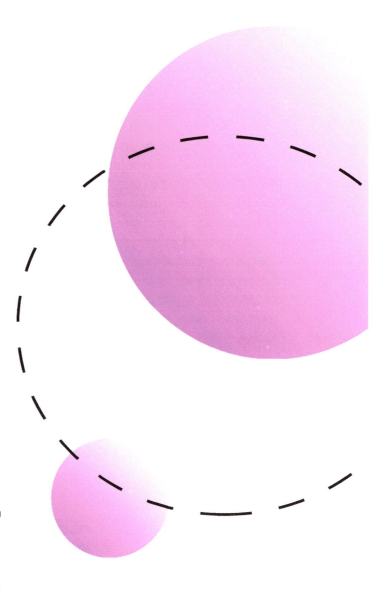

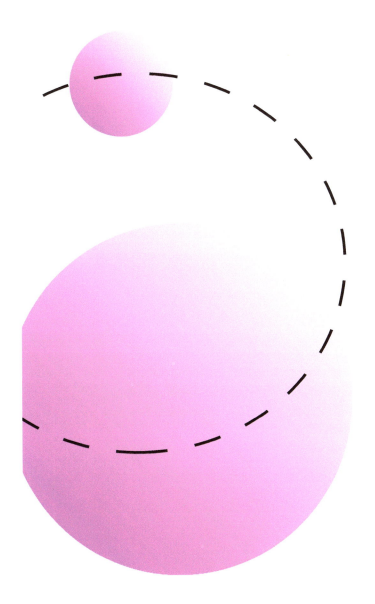

Overall, AI applications in environmental control offer a range of benefits for data center operators, including improved equipment reliability, reduced energy consumption, and enhanced operational efficiency. By harnessing the power of AI, data centers can achieve optimal environmental conditions, maximize resource utilization, and future-proof their operations against potential challenges. As AI continues to evolve, its role in environmental control will only become more critical in ensuring the success and sustainability of data center operations.

Enhancing Cooling Efficiency with AI

In today's fast-paced world, data centers play a crucial role in storing, managing, and processing vast amounts of information. However, one of the biggest challenges faced by data centers is managing the heat generated by servers and other equipment. Inefficient cooling systems can lead to overheating, which can result in equipment failures and downtime. This is where Artificial Intelligence (AI) comes in to revolutionize cooling efficiency in data centers.

AI-powered cooling and environmental control systems can significantly enhance the efficiency of cooling operations in data centers. By utilizing AI algorithms, these systems can analyze real-time data from sensors and adjust cooling settings accordingly to optimize energy consumption and maintain the ideal temperature for equipment. This not only improves the overall performance of the data center but also reduces energy costs and carbon footprint.

Moreover, AI-driven predictive maintenance for data center equipment can help prevent potential cooling system failures by detecting issues before they escalate. By analyzing historical data and performance patterns, AI algorithms can identify anomalies and predict when equipment is likely to fail. This proactive approach to maintenance not only minimizes downtime but also extends the lifespan of cooling systems, ultimately saving costs for data center operators.

AI-based security monitoring and threat detection can also play a vital role in enhancing cooling efficiency in data centers. By continuously monitoring network traffic and analyzing patterns, AI algorithms can detect potential security threats and breaches that could impact the cooling system. By identifying and responding to these threats in real-time, data center operators can ensure the integrity of their cooling systems and prevent any disruptions to operations.

In addition, AI-driven workload optimization and resource allocation can help data centers maximize the efficiency of their cooling systems. By analyzing workload patterns and resource demands, AI algorithms can dynamically allocate resources to optimize cooling efficiency based on real-time demand. This ensures that cooling systems are not overworked or underutilized, leading to improved performance and energy savings for data center operators.

Overall, AI innovations are transforming the way cooling systems operate in data centers. By leveraging AI technologies for predictive maintenance, security monitoring, workload optimization, and resource allocation, data center operators can enhance cooling efficiency, reduce energy costs, and improve overall performance. With AI-powered solutions, data centers can stay ahead of the curve and meet the demands of an increasingly data-driven world.

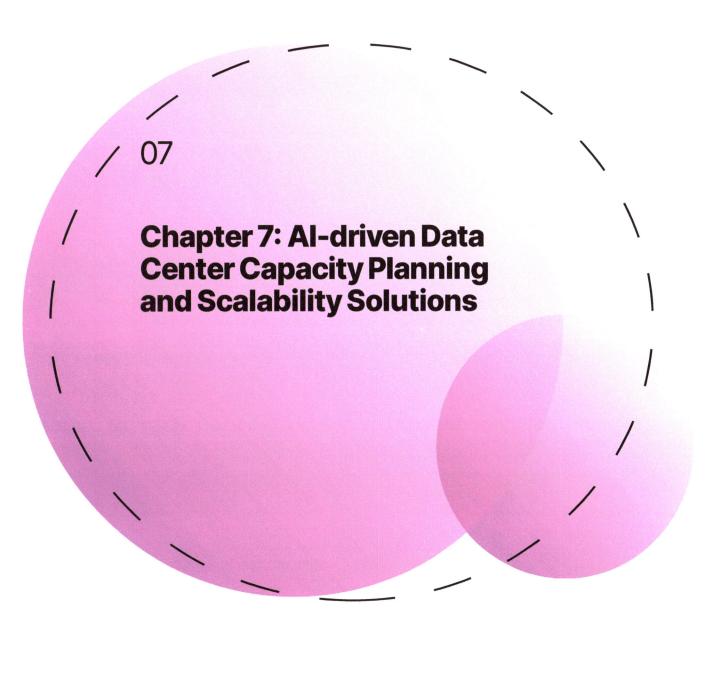

07

Chapter 7: AI-driven Data Center Capacity Planning and Scalability Solutions

Capacity Planning Challenges in Data Centers

Capacity planning in data centers is a crucial aspect of ensuring smooth operations and optimal performance. However, there are several challenges that professionals in the field need to be aware of and address effectively. One of the main challenges is the dynamic nature of data center workloads. With the increasing adoption of AI technologies and the growing demand for data processing power, workloads can vary significantly, making it difficult to accurately predict future capacity needs.

Another challenge is the complexity of modern data center infrastructures. With the proliferation of virtualization, cloud computing, and edge computing technologies, data centers are becoming more distributed and heterogeneous. This complexity can make it challenging to effectively plan for capacity requirements and ensure optimal resource allocation.

In addition, data centers are constantly evolving, with new technologies and hardware being introduced regularly. This rapid pace of change can make it difficult to keep up with capacity planning requirements and ensure that data center resources are being utilized efficiently. Professionals in the field need to stay updated on the latest trends and technologies to effectively plan for future capacity needs.

Furthermore, data center capacity planning is not just about adding more servers or storage units. It also involves optimizing energy consumption, cooling systems, and environmental controls to ensure optimal performance and efficiency. AI-powered solutions can help professionals in this field by providing predictive analytics and real-time monitoring to optimize energy usage and cooling systems, thereby reducing costs and improving overall efficiency.

Overall, capacity planning challenges in data centers require professionals to stay proactive, flexible, and innovative in their approach. By leveraging AI technologies and staying abreast of the latest trends, data center professionals can effectively address these challenges and ensure that their data centers are equipped to handle the demands of today's digital economy.

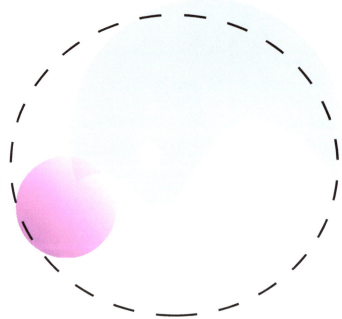

AI Models for Scalability Planning

In the ever-evolving world of data centers, scalability planning is a crucial aspect that cannot be overlooked. As data centers continue to grow in size and complexity, the need for efficient and effective scalability planning becomes more apparent. This is where AI models come into play, offering innovative solutions to help data center professionals optimize their infrastructure for future growth.

AI models for scalability planning leverage advanced algorithms and machine learning techniques to analyze historical data, predict future trends, and recommend optimal strategies for scaling up or down based on current and projected demands. By harnessing the power of AI, data center professionals can gain valuable insights into their infrastructure's capacity utilization, performance metrics, and resource allocation, allowing them to make informed decisions that maximize efficiency and minimize downtime.

One of the key benefits of using AI models for scalability planning is the ability to automate the process of capacity planning and resource allocation. By continuously monitoring and analyzing data center performance metrics in real-time, AI models can dynamically adjust resources to match workload demands, ensuring optimal performance and scalability at all times. This proactive approach not only improves efficiency but also reduces the risk of underutilization or overprovisioning, ultimately saving time and resources for data center professionals.

Furthermore, AI models can also help data center professionals identify potential bottlenecks, vulnerabilities, and performance issues before they escalate into critical problems. By leveraging AI-driven anomaly detection and performance monitoring tools, data center professionals can proactively address issues and implement corrective measures to prevent downtime and ensure uninterrupted operations. This proactive approach to maintenance and monitoring can significantly enhance the reliability and resilience of data center infrastructure, ultimately improving overall uptime and customer satisfaction.

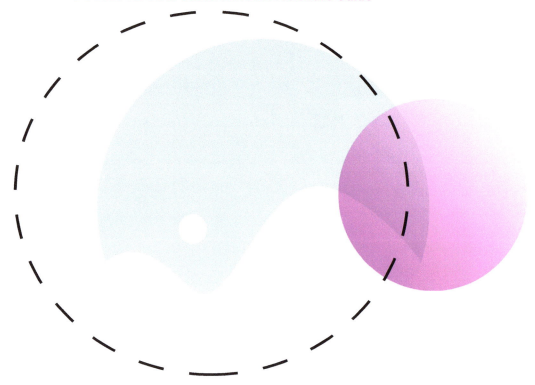

In conclusion, AI models for scalability planning are revolutionizing the way data center professionals approach capacity planning, resource allocation, and performance optimization. By harnessing the power of AI, data center professionals can gain valuable insights, automate critical tasks, and proactively address issues to ensure optimal scalability and efficiency. As data centers continue to evolve and grow in complexity, AI-driven solutions will play an increasingly important role in helping professionals navigate the challenges of scalability planning and ensure the long-term success of their infrastructure.

Ensuring Data Center Scalability with AI

In today's rapidly evolving technology landscape, data centers are facing increasing pressure to scale up and meet the growing demands of businesses and consumers. One of the key challenges that data center professionals face is ensuring scalability while maintaining efficiency and reliability. This is where artificial intelligence (AI) comes into play, offering innovative solutions to help data centers adapt and expand seamlessly.

AI-powered energy optimization for data centers is crucial in reducing operational costs and carbon footprint. By leveraging AI algorithms, data center professionals can analyze energy consumption patterns and optimize cooling systems to reduce energy wastage. This not only results in cost savings but also contributes to sustainability efforts, making data centers more environmentally friendly.

AI-driven predictive maintenance for data center equipment is another essential aspect of ensuring scalability. By using AI to analyze data from sensors and equipment performance metrics, data center professionals can predict potential failures before they occur. This proactive approach to maintenance helps prevent costly downtime and ensures the smooth operation of data center infrastructure.

AI-based security monitoring and threat detection for data centers are critical in safeguarding sensitive data and preventing cyberattacks. AI algorithms can analyze network traffic patterns and detect anomalies in real-time, allowing data center professionals to respond swiftly to potential security threats. This proactive approach to cybersecurity is essential in maintaining the integrity and confidentiality of data stored in data centers.

AI-driven workload optimization and resource allocation for data centers play a vital role in maximizing efficiency and performance. By using AI algorithms to analyze workload patterns and resource usage, data center professionals can optimize resource allocation to meet the demands of varying workloads. This dynamic approach to resource management ensures that data centers can scale up or down as needed without compromising performance.

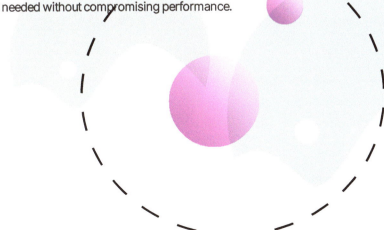

In conclusion, AI innovations are revolutionizing the way data centers operate, offering scalable solutions that enhance efficiency, reliability, and security. From energy optimization to predictive maintenance, security monitoring, workload optimization, and resource allocation, AI is transforming the data center landscape. By embracing AI technologies, data center professionals can ensure scalability and adaptability in the face of evolving business needs and technological advancements.

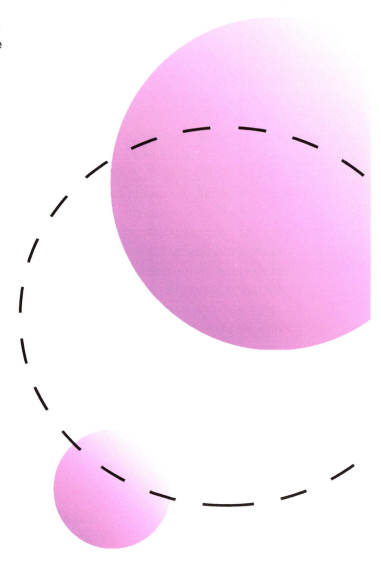

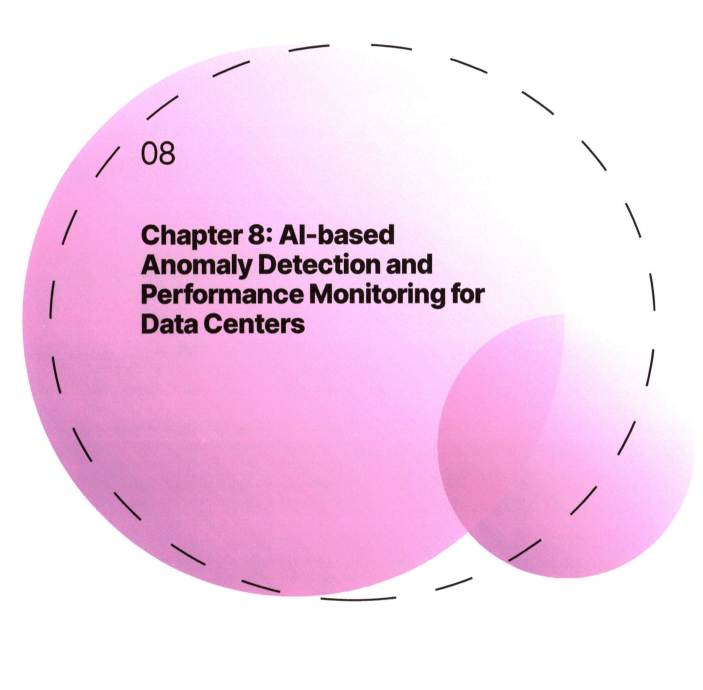

Chapter 8: AI-based Anomaly Detection and Performance Monitoring for Data Centers

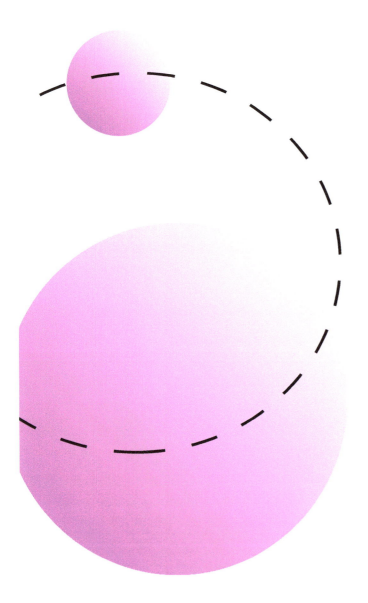

Anomalies in Data Center Operations

In the fast-paced world of data center operations, anomalies can arise that have the potential to disrupt the efficiency and effectiveness of these critical facilities. These anomalies, if left undetected or unaddressed, can lead to costly downtime, reduced performance, and increased security risks. In this subchapter, we will explore some of the key anomalies that can occur in data center operations and discuss how AI innovations can help professionals in the industry mitigate these risks.

One common anomaly in data center operations is unexpected spikes in energy consumption. These spikes can be caused by a variety of factors, such as equipment malfunctions, inefficient cooling systems, or changes in workload demands. AI-powered energy optimization solutions can help data center operators identify and address these spikes in real-time, ensuring that energy is being used efficiently and cost-effectively.

Another critical anomaly that data center professionals must be vigilant about is equipment failure. Predictive maintenance powered by AI algorithms can help detect early warning signs of potential equipment failures, allowing operators to schedule timely maintenance and avoid unplanned downtime. By leveraging AI-driven predictive maintenance tools, data center professionals can proactively manage equipment health and minimize the risk of costly disruptions.

Security monitoring and threat detection are also paramount concerns for data center operators, as these facilities house sensitive data and critical infrastructure. AI-based security monitoring solutions can continuously analyze network traffic, detect unusual patterns, and identify potential threats in real-time. By deploying AI-driven security monitoring and threat detection systems, professionals can enhance the resilience of their data centers and protect against cyber attacks.

In addition to security threats, data center professionals must also contend with performance anomalies that can affect the overall efficiency of their operations. AI-based anomaly detection and performance monitoring tools can analyze large volumes of data to identify deviations from normal behavior and pinpoint potential performance issues. By leveraging AI-driven anomaly detection solutions, professionals can proactively address performance anomalies and optimize the overall efficiency of their data center operations.

In conclusion, anomalies in data center operations pose significant risks to the efficiency, security, and performance of these critical facilities. By harnessing the power of AI innovations, professionals in the industry can detect, mitigate, and prevent anomalies in real-time, ensuring the smooth and reliable operation of their data centers. From energy optimization and predictive maintenance to security monitoring and performance optimization, AI technologies offer a wide range of solutions to help data center professionals address anomalies and enhance the resilience of their operations.

AI Techniques for Anomaly Detection

In the realm of data centers, anomaly detection is a crucial aspect of maintaining optimal performance and security. Artificial Intelligence (AI) techniques have revolutionized the way anomalies are detected and addressed in data centers, providing professionals with advanced tools and insights to ensure smooth operations. One of the key AI techniques for anomaly detection in data centers is machine learning. Machine learning algorithms can analyze vast amounts of data in real-time to identify patterns and anomalies that may indicate potential issues. By training these algorithms on historical data, data center professionals can proactively detect anomalies before they escalate into major problems.

Another AI technique for anomaly detection is deep learning. Deep learning algorithms, such as neural networks, are capable of detecting complex patterns and anomalies in data that may be missed by traditional methods. By leveraging deep learning techniques, data center professionals can enhance their anomaly detection capabilities and improve overall performance and security.

Furthermore, AI-powered anomaly detection systems can continuously learn and adapt to new data patterns, allowing for more accurate and efficient anomaly detection over time. These systems can automatically adjust their algorithms based on new data inputs, ensuring that data center professionals stay ahead of potential issues and threats.

Overall, AI techniques for anomaly detection in data centers offer professionals a powerful set of tools to enhance performance, security, and efficiency. By leveraging machine learning, deep learning, and AI-powered anomaly detection systems, data center professionals can proactively detect and address anomalies, leading to improved operations and reduced downtime. In the rapidly evolving landscape of data centers, AI innovations are essential for staying ahead of the curve and ensuring optimal performance and security.

Monitoring Performance with AI

In today's fast-paced world of data centers, monitoring performance is crucial to ensuring optimal efficiency and reliability. With the advancements in artificial intelligence (AI) technology, professionals in the field now have powerful tools at their disposal to help them track and analyze performance metrics in real-time. This subchapter will delve into the various ways in which AI can be leveraged to monitor performance in data centers, providing valuable insights and predictive capabilities to help professionals stay ahead of potential issues. One of the key benefits of using AI for performance monitoring in data centers is the ability to detect anomalies and potential problems before they escalate into serious issues. By analyzing vast amounts of data from various sources, AI algorithms can identify patterns and trends that may indicate a problem is brewing. This proactive approach to monitoring can help professionals take preemptive action to address issues before they impact the overall performance of the data center.

AI-powered energy optimization is another area where professionals can benefit from advanced performance monitoring. By leveraging AI algorithms to analyze energy consumption patterns and identify opportunities for optimization, professionals can reduce costs and improve efficiency. From adjusting cooling systems to optimizing workload distribution, AI can help data centers operate at peak performance while minimizing energy usage.

In addition to energy optimization, AI-driven predictive maintenance can also play a crucial role in monitoring performance in data centers. By analyzing equipment data and identifying potential maintenance needs before they occur, professionals can prevent downtime and extend the lifespan of critical assets. This proactive approach to maintenance can help data centers operate smoothly and efficiently, reducing the risk of costly disruptions.

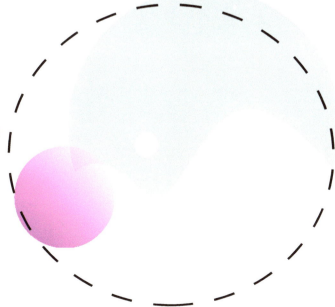

AI-based security monitoring and threat detection are also essential components of performance monitoring in data centers. With the increasing threat of cyberattacks and data breaches, professionals need to be vigilant in monitoring their systems for any signs of unauthorized access or suspicious activity. AI algorithms can help automate this process, flagging potential threats and helping professionals respond swiftly to protect sensitive data and maintain the security of the data center.

Overall, AI offers a wide range of capabilities for monitoring performance in data centers, from optimizing energy usage to detecting anomalies and potential threats. By leveraging AI technology, professionals can stay ahead of potential issues and ensure the smooth operation of their data centers. With the right tools and strategies in place, professionals can harness the power of AI to drive efficiency, reliability, and security in their data center operations.

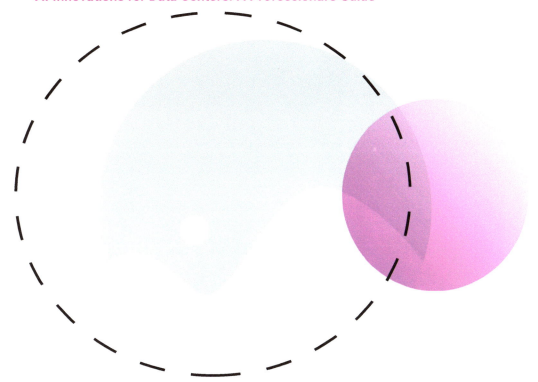

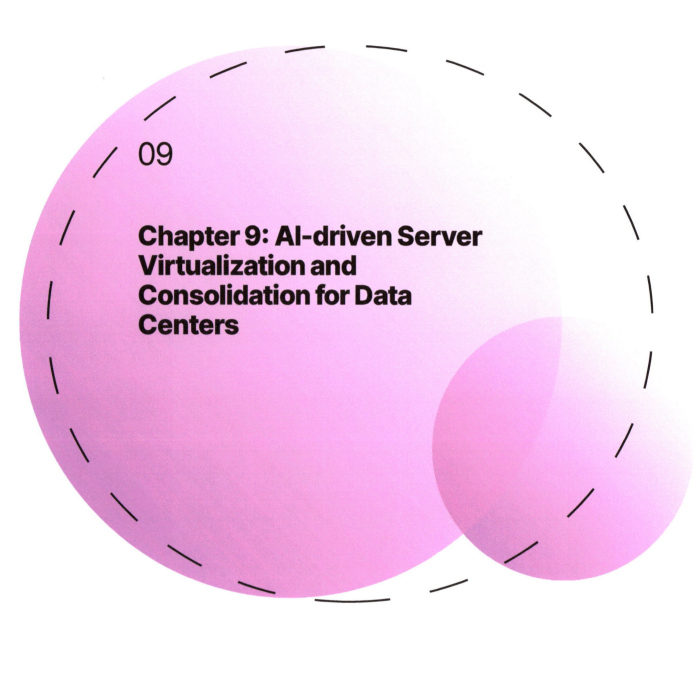

09

Chapter 9: AI-driven Server Virtualization and Consolidation for Data Centers

Server Virtualization Benefits

Server virtualization is a technology that allows multiple virtual servers to run on a single physical server. This means that one physical server can be divided into multiple virtual servers, each of which can run its own operating system and applications. This technology offers a number of benefits for data centers, making it a popular choice for many organizations looking to optimize their server infrastructure.

One of the key benefits of server virtualization is increased efficiency. By running multiple virtual servers on a single physical server, organizations can make better use of their hardware resources and reduce the number of physical servers needed in their data centers. This can lead to cost savings on hardware, power, cooling, and maintenance, making server virtualization an attractive option for organizations looking to reduce their IT costs.

Another benefit of server virtualization is improved flexibility and scalability. Virtual servers can be easily provisioned, moved, and scaled up or down to meet changing business needs. This allows organizations to quickly adapt to changing workloads and demands, without the need to purchase and deploy new physical servers. This flexibility can help organizations improve their agility and responsiveness, allowing them to better meet the needs of their customers and stakeholders.

Server virtualization also offers improved reliability and availability. Virtual servers can be easily backed up, replicated, and migrated to other physical servers in the event of hardware failure or maintenance. This can help organizations minimize downtime and ensure that their critical applications and services remain available and accessible to users. By virtualizing their servers, organizations can improve their overall resilience and reduce the risk of costly outages.

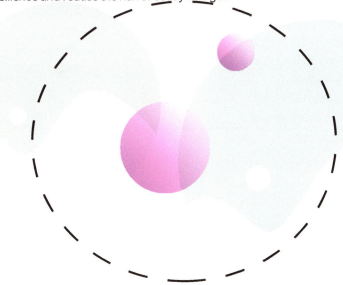

In addition to these benefits, server virtualization can also help organizations improve their security and compliance. Virtual servers can be isolated from each other, providing an additional layer of protection against security breaches and unauthorized access. Virtual servers can also be easily monitored and audited, helping organizations ensure that their systems are compliant with industry regulations and best practices. By leveraging the power of AI-driven server virtualization, organizations can enhance the security, efficiency, and flexibility of their data centers, enabling them to better meet the needs of their business and customers.

AI-driven Consolidation Strategies

In the fast-paced world of data centers, the need for efficient and effective consolidation strategies has never been greater. With the advent of Artificial Intelligence (AI) technologies, professionals in the field now have access to powerful tools that can revolutionize the way data centers are managed and optimized. In this subchapter, we will explore AI-driven consolidation strategies that can help data center professionals streamline operations, improve efficiency, and reduce costs.

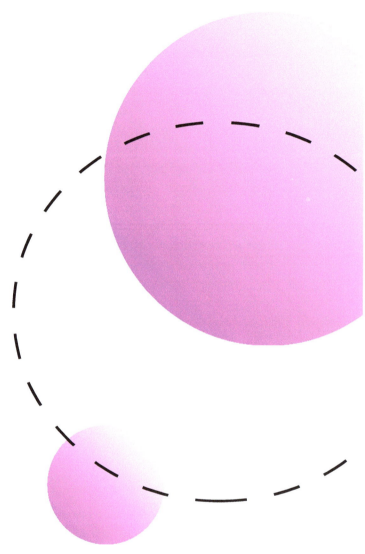

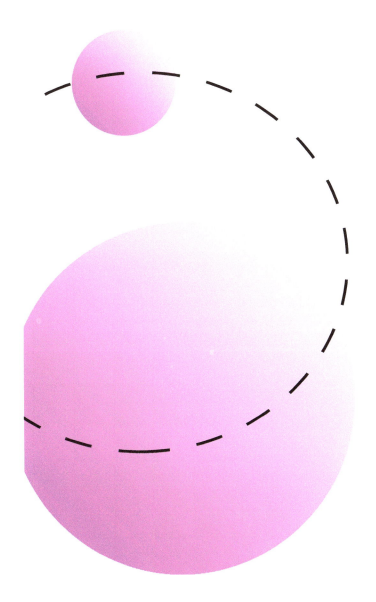

One of the key benefits of AI-driven consolidation strategies is the ability to optimize energy usage within data centers. By leveraging AI algorithms to analyze and predict energy consumption patterns, data center operators can identify opportunities to reduce energy waste and lower costs. AI-powered energy optimization solutions can automatically adjust cooling and power usage based on real-time data, ensuring that resources are used efficiently without compromising performance.

In addition to energy optimization, AI-driven predictive maintenance for data center equipment can help prevent costly downtime and equipment failures. By monitoring equipment performance and identifying potential issues before they occur, AI algorithms can schedule maintenance tasks proactively, minimizing the risk of unexpected failures. This proactive approach to maintenance can help data center professionals avoid costly repairs and keep operations running smoothly.

AI-based security monitoring and threat detection is another critical aspect of consolidation strategies for data centers. With the increasing number of cyber threats targeting data centers, it is essential to have robust security measures in place. AI-powered security solutions can analyze vast amounts of data in real-time to detect anomalies and potential security breaches, providing data center professionals with the tools they need to respond quickly and effectively to threats.

Furthermore, AI-driven workload optimization and resource allocation can help data center professionals maximize the efficiency of their infrastructure. By analyzing workload patterns and resource usage data, AI algorithms can dynamically allocate resources based on demand, ensuring that applications run smoothly and efficiently. This intelligent approach to resource management can help data center operators optimize performance and reduce costs by eliminating unnecessary resource waste.

In conclusion, AI-driven consolidation strategies offer data center professionals a powerful set of tools to optimize operations, improve efficiency, and reduce costs. From energy optimization and predictive maintenance to security monitoring and resource allocation, AI technologies can revolutionize the way data centers are managed and maintained. By leveraging AI solutions, data center professionals can stay ahead of the curve and ensure that their infrastructure is running at peak performance.

Implementing Server Virtualization with AI

Implementing server virtualization with AI is a game-changer for data centers looking to optimize their resources and increase efficiency. By harnessing the power of artificial intelligence, professionals can automate the process of virtualizing servers, leading to cost savings and improved performance.

One of the key benefits of implementing server virtualization with AI is the ability to optimize workload distribution and resource allocation. AI algorithms can analyze data in real-time and make intelligent decisions about where to allocate resources based on current demand. This ensures that servers are utilized to their full capacity, reducing the need for additional hardware and lowering energy costs.

AI-driven server virtualization also enables data centers to quickly adapt to changing workloads and scale up or down as needed. By constantly monitoring performance metrics and predicting future demands, AI can help data center professionals make proactive decisions about resource allocation and capacity planning. This flexibility is essential for data centers that need to respond quickly to fluctuating demands.

In addition to optimizing resource allocation, AI can also improve security monitoring and threat detection in virtualized server environments. By analyzing network traffic patterns and identifying anomalies, AI algorithms can detect potential security threats before they escalate. This proactive approach to security can help data centers prevent costly data breaches and ensure the integrity of their systems.

Overall, implementing server virtualization with AI is a powerful tool for data center professionals looking to increase efficiency, reduce costs, and improve security. By harnessing the capabilities of artificial intelligence, data centers can optimize resource allocation, scale up or down as needed, and enhance security monitoring. With AI-powered server virtualization, data centers can stay ahead of the curve and meet the demands of today's rapidly evolving digital landscape.

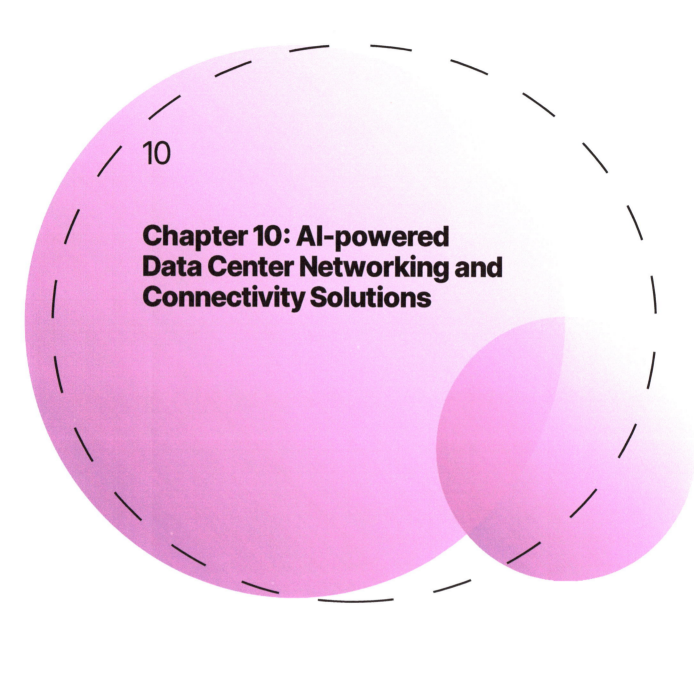

10

Chapter 10: AI-powered Data Center Networking and Connectivity Solutions

Networking Challenges in Data Centers

Networking challenges in data centers are a critical aspect that professionals in the field need to address in order to ensure optimal performance and efficiency. With the increasing complexity of data center environments and the growing demand for high-speed connectivity, networking challenges have become more prevalent than ever before. From ensuring seamless communication between servers and storage devices to managing virtualized networks and ensuring security protocols are in place, there are various hurdles that professionals must overcome to keep their data centers running smoothly.

One of the key networking challenges in data centers is scalability. As data centers continue to grow in size and complexity, the network infrastructure must be able to accommodate the increasing demands placed on it. This includes ensuring that networks can easily scale up or down based on changing requirements, without compromising performance or reliability. Professionals must also consider factors such as bandwidth limitations, network congestion, and latency issues when designing and implementing networking solutions in data centers.

Another major networking challenge in data centers is security. With the rise of cyber threats and attacks targeting data centers, professionals must implement robust security measures to protect sensitive data and prevent unauthorized access. This includes implementing encryption protocols, firewalls, intrusion detection systems, and other security mechanisms to safeguard the network infrastructure from potential threats. Professionals must also stay up-to-date on the latest security trends and technologies to ensure their data centers remain secure in the face of evolving threats.

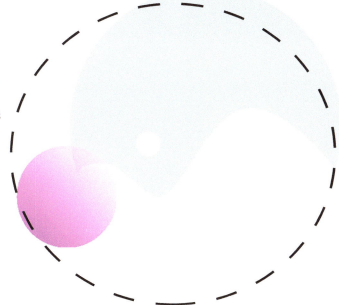

Additionally, professionals must address the challenge of network performance monitoring and optimization in data centers. This involves continuously monitoring network traffic, identifying bottlenecks and performance issues, and optimizing network configurations to ensure optimal performance and efficiency. By leveraging AI-driven solutions, professionals can automate the monitoring and optimization process, allowing them to proactively identify and address network performance issues before they impact overall data center operations.

In conclusion, networking challenges in data centers are complex and multifaceted, requiring professionals to stay vigilant and proactive in addressing them. By implementing scalable, secure, and optimized networking solutions, professionals can ensure that their data centers operate at peak performance and efficiency, enabling them to meet the growing demands of today's digital economy. With the right tools, technologies, and strategies in place, professionals can overcome these challenges and build resilient and agile networking infrastructures that support their data center operations effectively.

AI-driven Network Optimization

In the rapidly evolving world of data centers, the integration of artificial intelligence (AI) technology has revolutionized network optimization. AI-driven network optimization allows professionals to maximize the efficiency and performance of their data centers in ways that were previously unimaginable. By leveraging AI algorithms and machine learning capabilities, data center professionals can now proactively monitor, analyze, and adjust network configurations to meet the ever-changing demands of their operations.

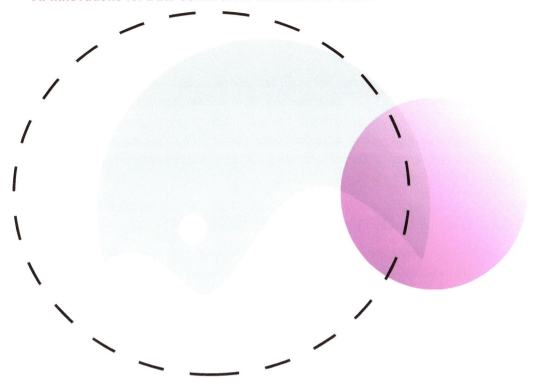

One key aspect of AI-driven network optimization is the ability to predict and prevent network bottlenecks before they occur. By analyzing historical data and real-time network traffic patterns, AI algorithms can identify potential congestion points and automatically adjust network configurations to alleviate these issues. This proactive approach not only improves network performance but also enhances overall data center efficiency by reducing downtime and optimizing resource utilization.

AI-powered energy optimization for data centers is another crucial aspect of network optimization. By analyzing energy consumption patterns, AI algorithms can identify opportunities for reducing energy waste and optimizing power usage. This not only leads to cost savings for data center operators but also contributes to sustainability efforts by reducing the carbon footprint of data center operations.

In addition to energy optimization, AI-driven predictive maintenance for data center equipment plays a vital role in network optimization. By analyzing equipment performance data and predicting potential failures, AI algorithms can help data center professionals proactively address maintenance issues before they escalate into costly downtime events. This predictive maintenance approach not only improves data center reliability but also extends the lifespan of critical equipment, ultimately leading to cost savings and operational efficiency.

Furthermore, AI-based security monitoring and threat detection for data centers are essential components of network optimization. By continuously monitoring network traffic and identifying potential security threats in real-time, AI algorithms can help data center professionals detect and mitigate cyber threats before they compromise data center operations. This proactive approach to cybersecurity not only enhances data center security but also ensures the integrity and confidentiality of sensitive data stored within the facility.

Enhancing Connectivity with AI

In today's rapidly evolving digital landscape, data centers play a crucial role in supporting the growing demands of various industries. As technology continues to advance, the need for efficient and effective data center management has never been more critical. One of the key ways in which data centers can enhance their operations is by leveraging the power of artificial intelligence (AI) to improve connectivity and optimize performance.

AI for data centers offers a wide range of benefits, including enhanced connectivity. By utilizing AI-powered networking and connectivity solutions, data centers can ensure seamless communication between servers, devices, and applications. AI algorithms can analyze network traffic patterns in real-time, identify potential bottlenecks, and optimize data routing to improve overall performance and reduce latency.

AI-powered energy optimization is another key aspect of enhancing connectivity in data centers. By leveraging AI algorithms to analyze energy consumption patterns, data centers can identify opportunities to optimize energy usage, reduce costs, and minimize environmental impact. AI-driven predictive maintenance for data center equipment can also help prevent downtime and ensure that critical systems remain operational.

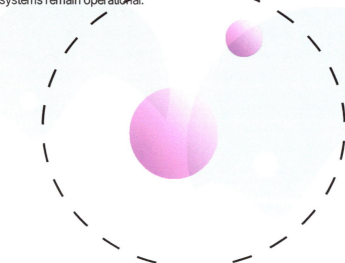

Security is a top priority for data centers, and AI-based security monitoring and threat detection solutions can help safeguard against cyber threats. By leveraging AI algorithms to analyze network traffic, detect anomalies, and identify potential security breaches, data centers can enhance their cybersecurity posture and protect sensitive data from unauthorized access.

In addition to security, AI-driven workload optimization and resource allocation can help data centers maximize efficiency and performance. By analyzing workload patterns, AI algorithms can dynamically allocate resources to ensure optimal performance for critical applications. AI-powered cooling and environmental control systems can also help data centers maintain optimal operating temperatures and reduce energy consumption.

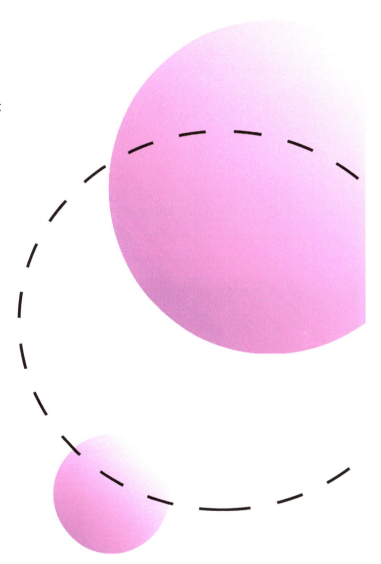

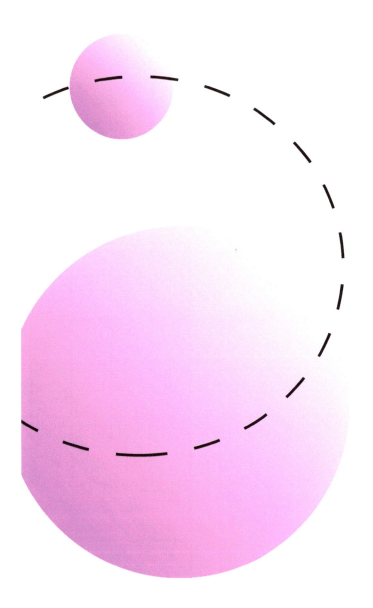

Overall, AI innovations are revolutionizing the way data centers operate and enhancing connectivity in ways that were previously unimaginable. By leveraging AI for data center management, professionals can optimize performance, improve security, and ensure seamless connectivity to support the growing demands of today's digital economy. AI-powered data center capacity planning and scalability solutions can help data centers adapt to changing demands and ensure that they can accommodate future growth. AI-based anomaly detection and performance monitoring solutions enable data center professionals to identify and address issues before they impact operations, while AI-driven disaster recovery and business continuity planning solutions can help data centers prepare for and mitigate potential disruptions. AI-driven server virtualization and consolidation solutions can help data centers optimize resource usage and reduce costs, while AI-powered data center networking and connectivity solutions can enhance communication and collaboration across the data center ecosystem.

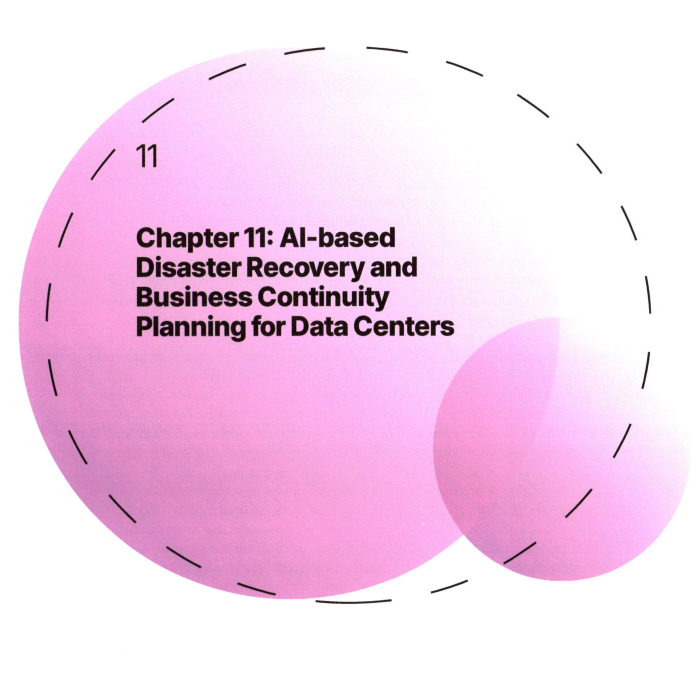

11

Chapter 11: AI-based Disaster Recovery and Business Continuity Planning for Data Centers

Importance of Disaster Recovery Planning

In the fast-paced world of data centers, disaster recovery planning is often overlooked or underestimated. However, the importance of disaster recovery planning cannot be overstated. In the event of a natural disaster, cyber attack, or equipment failure, having a solid disaster recovery plan in place can mean the difference between minimal downtime and a catastrophic loss of data and revenue. For professionals working in the realm of AI for data centers, disaster recovery planning should be a top priority to ensure the continued success and resilience of their operations.

AI-powered energy optimization for data centers is a critical component of disaster recovery planning. By utilizing AI algorithms to monitor and adjust energy consumption in real-time, data centers can ensure that they have enough power to keep critical systems running during a disaster. Additionally, AI-driven predictive maintenance for data center equipment can help prevent equipment failures before they occur, reducing the risk of downtime during a crisis. These AI technologies work hand-in-hand to keep data centers up and running, even in the face of a disaster.

AI-based security monitoring and threat detection for data centers are also essential elements of disaster recovery planning. In today's digital landscape, cyber attacks are a constant threat to data center operations. By leveraging AI to monitor for potential security breaches and detect anomalies in real-time, data centers can better protect their systems and data from malicious actors. In the event of a security breach, AI-driven threat detection can help data center professionals quickly identify and mitigate the threat, minimizing the impact on operations and data integrity.

AI-driven workload optimization and resource allocation for data centers play a crucial role in disaster recovery planning. By using AI algorithms to dynamically allocate resources based on workload demands, data centers can ensure that critical systems have the resources they need to function properly during and after a disaster. Additionally, AI-powered cooling and environmental control systems can help data centers maintain optimal operating conditions, even in the face of extreme weather or other environmental challenges. These AI technologies help data centers stay online and operational, even in the most challenging circumstances.

AI-driven data center capacity planning and scalability solutions are key components of disaster recovery planning. By using AI to predict future capacity needs and scale resources accordingly, data centers can ensure that they have the capacity to handle increased workloads during a disaster. Additionally, AI-based anomaly detection and performance monitoring can help data center professionals identify and address potential issues before they impact operations. By leveraging these AI technologies, data centers can better prepare for and respond to disasters, ensuring the continuity of operations and the protection of critical data.

AI Approaches to Business Continuity

In the ever-evolving landscape of data centers, ensuring business continuity is crucial for organizations to maintain operations and meet the demands of their customers. Artificial Intelligence (AI) is revolutionizing the way businesses approach disaster recovery and continuity planning, offering innovative solutions to mitigate risks and enhance resilience. AI-powered technologies are being increasingly utilized to streamline processes, optimize resources, and proactively address potential disruptions. One of the key AI approaches to business continuity is predictive maintenance for data center equipment. By leveraging AI algorithms and machine learning models, organizations can predict equipment failures before they occur, allowing for timely maintenance and minimizing downtime. This proactive approach not only reduces operational costs but also improves overall system reliability and performance.

AI-based security monitoring and threat detection are also critical components of business continuity planning for data centers. With the increasing sophistication of cyber threats, organizations need advanced security solutions that can detect and respond to potential breaches in real-time. AI-powered security systems can analyze vast amounts of data to identify anomalies and potential threats, enabling organizations to take proactive measures to safeguard their data and infrastructure. Additionally, AI-driven workload optimization and resource allocation play a significant role in ensuring business continuity in data centers. By dynamically allocating resources based on workload demands and performance metrics, organizations can optimize efficiency, minimize downtime, and maximize resource utilization. AI algorithms can also predict future workload patterns, allowing organizations to scale resources accordingly and adapt to changing business needs.

Furthermore, AI-powered cooling and environmental control systems are essential for maintaining optimal operating conditions in data centers. By continuously monitoring temperature, humidity, and airflow, AI systems can automatically adjust cooling systems to prevent overheating and ensure equipment reliability. This proactive approach not only extends the lifespan of equipment but also reduces energy consumption and operational costs.

In conclusion, AI innovations are transforming the way businesses approach disaster recovery and business continuity planning in data centers. By leveraging AI approaches such as predictive maintenance, security monitoring, workload optimization, and environmental control, organizations can enhance resilience, reduce risks, and ensure uninterrupted operations. As AI technologies continue to advance, businesses can stay ahead of potential disruptions and maintain a competitive edge in the rapidly evolving digital landscape.

Ensuring Data Center Resilience with AI

In the fast-paced world of data centers, ensuring resilience is crucial to maintaining operations and meeting business demands. With the advent of artificial intelligence (AI), data center professionals now have powerful tools at their disposal to enhance resilience and optimize performance. AI innovations are revolutionizing the way data centers operate, offering solutions that can predict and prevent downtime, optimize energy usage, and enhance security measures.

One key aspect of data center resilience is AI-powered energy optimization. By utilizing AI algorithms, data center operators can analyze real-time data on energy consumption and make adjustments to optimize efficiency. This not only reduces costs but also helps to minimize the environmental impact of data center operations. AI can also predict energy usage patterns and recommend strategies for reducing consumption during peak times, ensuring that data centers operate at peak efficiency.

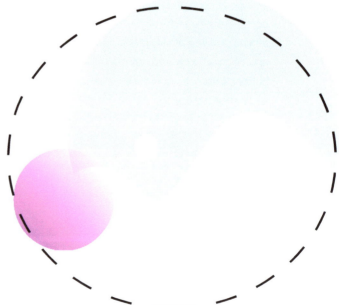

Another critical area where AI is making a significant impact is in predictive maintenance for data center equipment. By leveraging AI-driven analytics, data center professionals can monitor the health of equipment in real-time and predict potential failures before they occur. This proactive approach to maintenance not only reduces downtime but also extends the lifespan of critical equipment, saving time and money in the long run. AI can also recommend maintenance schedules based on the condition of equipment, ensuring that data centers operate smoothly without any unexpected disruptions.

In terms of security monitoring and threat detection, AI is revolutionizing the way data centers protect sensitive information and infrastructure. AI-based security systems can analyze vast amounts of data to identify potential threats and anomalies in real-time, allowing data center operators to respond quickly and effectively to potential security breaches. By continuously monitoring network traffic and analyzing patterns, AI can detect and mitigate threats before they escalate, safeguarding data center operations and ensuring the integrity of critical systems.

AI-driven workload optimization and resource allocation are also key factors in ensuring data center resilience. By using AI algorithms to analyze workload patterns and resource usage, data center professionals can optimize performance and allocate resources more efficiently. This not only improves the overall performance of data centers but also ensures that resources are utilized in the most cost-effective manner. AI can also predict future workload demands and recommend strategies for scaling resources up or down as needed, ensuring that data centers can adapt to changing business requirements.

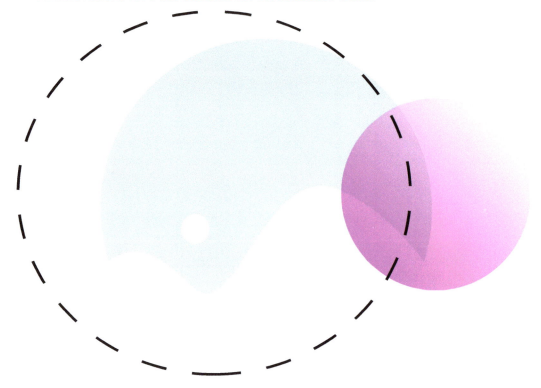

In conclusion, AI innovations are transforming the way data centers operate, offering powerful tools to enhance resilience and optimize performance. From energy optimization and predictive maintenance to security monitoring and workload optimization, AI is revolutionizing every aspect of data center operations. By embracing AI technologies, data center professionals can ensure that their facilities operate at peak efficiency, minimizing downtime, reducing costs, and enhancing security measures. The future of data center resilience is AI-driven, and those who embrace these innovations will be well-positioned to meet the challenges of tomorrow's digital landscape.

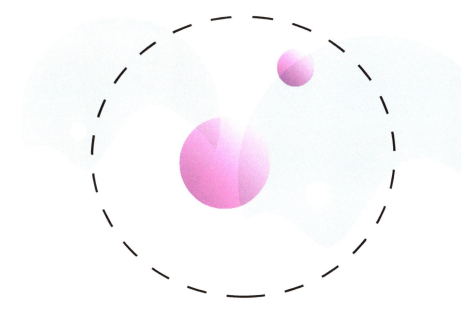

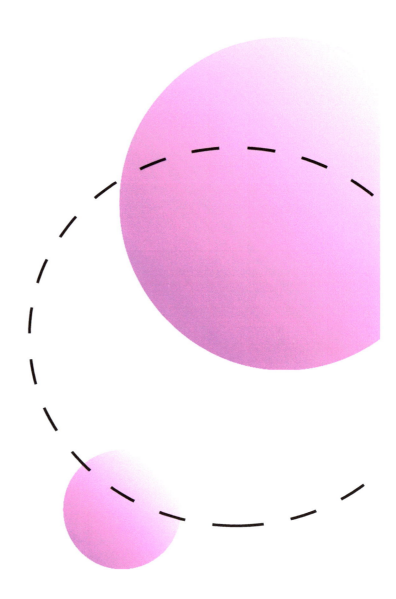

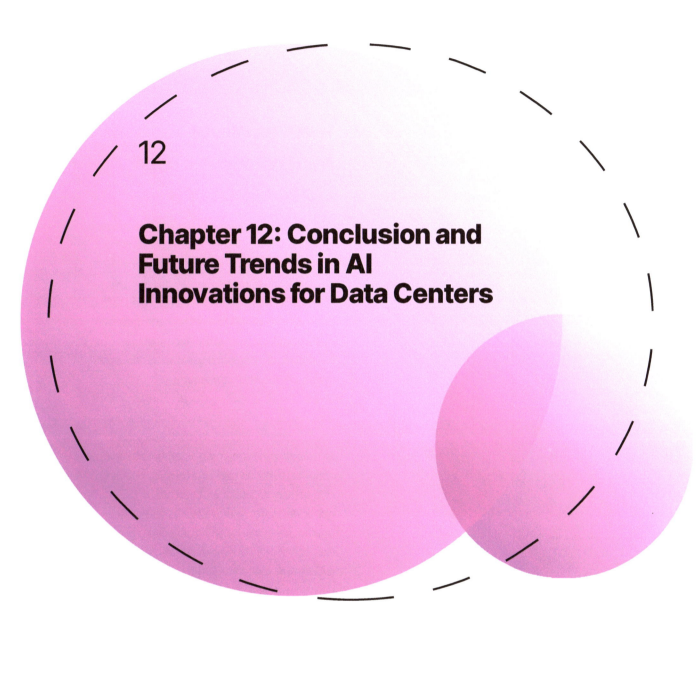

12

Chapter 12: Conclusion and Future Trends in AI Innovations for Data Centers

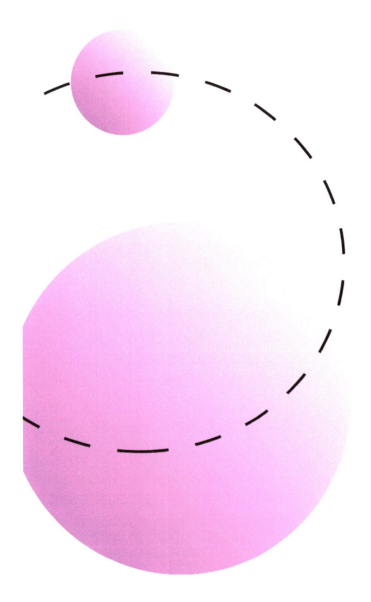

Recap of AI Innovations for Data Centers

In this subchapter titled "Recap of AI Innovations for Data Centers," we will review some of the key advancements in artificial intelligence (AI) that are revolutionizing the way data centers operate. These innovations are designed to help professionals optimize energy usage, improve maintenance practices, enhance security monitoring, and streamline resource allocation in data center environments.

One of the most exciting developments in AI for data centers is the emergence of AI-powered energy optimization solutions. These tools leverage machine learning algorithms to analyze historical data and real-time metrics, enabling data center professionals to identify opportunities for energy savings and reduce operational costs. By optimizing energy usage, data centers can operate more efficiently and reduce their carbon footprint.

Another critical area of innovation is AI-driven predictive maintenance for data center equipment. By utilizing AI algorithms to analyze equipment performance data, professionals can anticipate potential issues before they occur and schedule maintenance proactively. This approach minimizes downtime, extends the lifespan of equipment, and ultimately enhances the overall reliability of data center operations.

In terms of security monitoring and threat detection, AI-based solutions are becoming increasingly essential for safeguarding data center environments. These tools use advanced machine learning algorithms to detect anomalies, identify potential threats, and respond to security incidents in real-time. By leveraging AI-driven security monitoring, data center professionals can enhance their cybersecurity posture and protect sensitive data from malicious actors.

Furthermore, AI-driven workload optimization and resource allocation tools are transforming the way data centers manage their computing resources. By analyzing workload patterns and performance metrics, these AI-powered solutions can automatically adjust resource allocations to meet changing demand levels. This dynamic approach to resource management improves efficiency, reduces wastage, and ensures optimal performance across data center environments.

Overall, the integration of AI technologies in data centers is enabling professionals to enhance operational efficiency, improve maintenance practices, strengthen security measures, and optimize resource allocations. As AI continues to evolve, data center professionals can expect even more innovative solutions to emerge, further transforming the way data centers operate and deliver services to their users.

Emerging Trends in AI Technologies

In recent years, the field of Artificial Intelligence (AI) has seen tremendous growth and innovation, especially in the realm of data centers. As data centers continue to play a crucial role in modern businesses, AI technologies are being increasingly utilized to optimize their operations and enhance their efficiency. In this subchapter, we will explore some of the emerging trends in AI technologies that are revolutionizing the way data centers are managed and maintained.

One of the key trends in AI technologies for data centers is AI-powered energy optimization. By leveraging AI algorithms and machine learning techniques, data center operators can analyze energy consumption patterns and optimize their energy usage to reduce costs and minimize environmental impact. AI-driven predictive maintenance is another important trend in data center management, enabling proactive monitoring and maintenance of equipment to prevent costly downtime and ensure optimal performance.

Security is a top priority for data centers, and AI technologies are being increasingly used for security monitoring and threat detection. AI-based security solutions can analyze vast amounts of data in real-time to identify potential threats and vulnerabilities, helping data center operators to respond quickly and effectively to cyber-attacks. AI-driven workload optimization and resource allocation is also a key trend in data center management, enabling operators to dynamically allocate resources based on workload demands and optimize performance. Cooling and environmental control systems are critical for maintaining the optimal operating conditions in data centers, and AI-powered solutions are revolutionizing the way these systems are managed. AI algorithms can analyze environmental data and adjust cooling systems in real-time to ensure optimal performance and energy efficiency. Additionally, AI-driven data center capacity planning and scalability solutions enable operators to predict future capacity needs and plan for growth effectively.

In conclusion, AI technologies are transforming the way data centers are managed and operated, offering innovative solutions for energy optimization, predictive maintenance, security monitoring, workload optimization, cooling systems management, capacity planning, and scalability. As data centers continue to evolve and grow in complexity, AI technologies will play an increasingly important role in ensuring their efficiency, reliability, and security. For professionals in the data center industry, staying informed about these emerging trends in AI technologies is essential for staying ahead of the curve and driving innovation in their organizations.

Future Outlook for AI in Data Center Operations

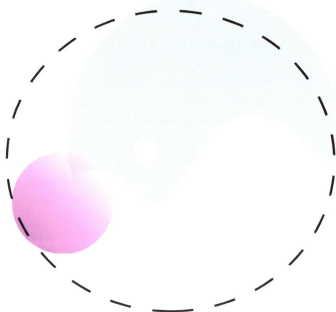

The future outlook for AI in data center operations is incredibly promising, with new innovations and advancements on the horizon that will revolutionize the way data centers are managed. AI for data centers is already being used to optimize energy consumption, predict equipment failures, monitor security threats, and optimize workloads and resource allocation. As AI technology continues to evolve, we can expect to see even more advanced applications in data center operations.

One of the most exciting developments in AI for data centers is the use of AI-powered energy optimization systems. These systems use machine learning algorithms to analyze data center energy usage and identify ways to reduce consumption without sacrificing performance. By optimizing energy usage, data centers can reduce their carbon footprint and save on operating costs.

Another key area where AI is making a big impact in data center operations is predictive maintenance. AI-driven predictive maintenance systems can analyze data from equipment sensors to predict when a piece of equipment is likely to fail, allowing data center operators to proactively address issues before they cause downtime. This can help data centers avoid costly repairs and minimize downtime, ensuring that critical operations continue running smoothly.

AI-based security monitoring and threat detection are also becoming increasingly important in data center operations. As cyber threats continue to evolve and become more sophisticated, data center operators need advanced tools to detect and respond to security breaches. AI-powered security systems can analyze vast amounts of data in real-time to identify potential threats and take action to mitigate risks before they escalate.

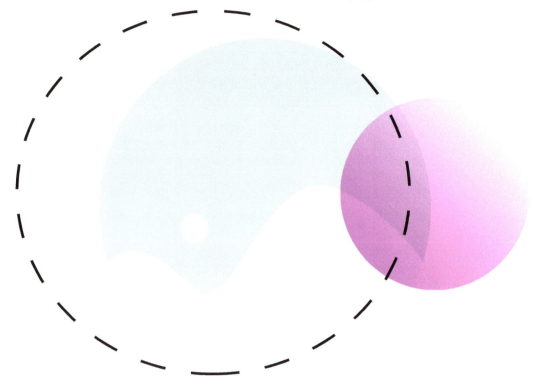

In addition to energy optimization, predictive maintenance, and security monitoring, AI is also being used to optimize workload and resource allocation in data centers. By analyzing data on workload patterns and resource usage, AI systems can help data center operators allocate resources more efficiently, ensuring that workloads are distributed evenly and resources are used effectively. This can help data centers maximize performance and minimize wasted resources.

Overall, the future outlook for AI in data center operations is bright, with new innovations and advancements on the horizon that will continue to improve the efficiency, reliability, and security of data centers. As AI technology continues to evolve, data center operators can expect to see even more advanced applications that will help them optimize energy usage, predict equipment failures, monitor security threats, and optimize workload and resource allocation. By embracing AI innovations in data center operations, professionals can stay ahead of the curve and ensure that their data centers are equipped to meet the challenges of tomorrow.

www.ingramcontent.com/pod-product-compliance
Lightning Source LLC
LaVergne TN
LVHW060159050326
832903LV00017B/362